natural English

elementary student's book

Ruth Gairns & Stuart Redman

OXFORD
UNIVERSITY PRESS

contents

units one to eight

contents

4

units nine to fourteen

natural English website
www.oup.com/elt/naturalenglish
interactive games and
exercises, and selected
web links

also available
reading & writing
skills resource book
complements the *natural
English* reading and writing
syllabuses

– an extra reading and
  writing lesson for every
  unit of the student's book
– material related to the
  student's book by topic
– develops 'real life' reading
  and writing skills useful
  for work or study
– advice on text types and
  skills

one

students

tick ✓ when you know this

natural English
- [ ] saying hello
- [ ] *What's your phone number?*
- [ ] *How are you?*
- [ ] *Would you like ...?*
- [ ] asking for help

grammar
- [ ] *be* positive and negative
- [ ] *a / an*
- [ ] questions with *be*

vocabulary
- [ ] jobs
- [ ] countries and nationalities
- [ ] numbers (1)
- [ ] drinks

listening
how to ... say hello

lead-in

1 **1.1** **natural English** Jennifer and Marc meet at Oxford International Business College. Listen and complete with *Hi* or *Hello*.

Jennifer

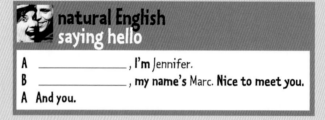

natural English
saying hello

A _____ , I'm Jennifer.
B _____ , my name's Marc. **Nice to meet you.**
A And you.

2 **pronunciation** Listen again. What's the pronunciation of *meet you*? Practise the conversation with a partner.

3 Stand up and say hello to five students you don't know.

Marc

OXFORD INTERNATIONAL BUSINESS COLLEGE

COURSE PROGRAMMES

listen to this

tune in

1 Read the sentences. With a partner, write J (Jennifer) or M (Marc).

I'm from France.

I'm from Canada.

I'm 21 (twenty-one).

I'm a teacher.

I'm a student.

I'm not married. / I'm single.

I'm married.

2 🎧 1.2 Listen to the first part. Where's Marc from in France?

listen carefully

3 Listen to the whole conversation. Check the answers to **exercise 1.**

listening challenge

4 🎧 1.3 Listen. Underline the correct answer.

1 Jennifer's husband is called Tim / Jim.
2 He's a business teacher / an English teacher.
3 He's a teacher at the business school / university.
4 He's from Canada / America.

listen again with the **tapescript** *p.146*

grammar *be positive and negative*

1 Say four things about Marc.

example Marc's from France, and **he's** ... /hiːz/

2 Say four things about Jennifer.

example Jennifer's from Canada, and **she's**... /ʃiːz/

3 Complete the table.

FULL FORM	CONTRACTION
I **am** a teacher.	_____ a teacher.
He **is** a doctor.	_____ a doctor.
She **is** a student.	_____ a student.
NEGATIVE	SHORT ANSWERS
_____ a teacher.	Yes, I am. / No, I'm not.
He **isn't** (is not) a doctor.	Yes, he is. / No, he isn't.
_____ a student.	Yes, she is. / No, she isn't.

4 With a partner, make sentences about Jennifer, Marc, and Tim. Use the words in the circles.

examples Jennifer **isn't** from Ottowa, she's from Toronto.
Tim's married.

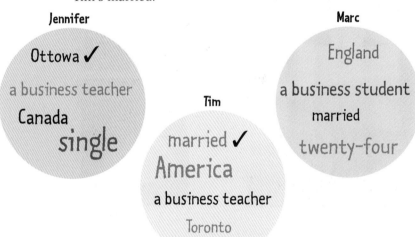

Jennifer
Ottowa ✔
a business teacher
Canada
single

Tim
married ✔
America
a business teacher
Toronto

Marc
England
a business student
married
twenty-four

5 With your partner, ask and answer the questions. Say:
Yes, he / she is.   *No, he / she isn't.*

1 Is Marc from France?
2 Is Jennifer a student?
3 Is Marc from Marseille?
4 Is Jennifer from San Francisco?
5 Is Jennifer married to Tim?
6 Is Marc married?

6 Write three questions to ask your partner.

example Is Tim from Canada?

7 Think of two sentences about yourself. Tell your partner.

go to **language reference** *and* **practice exercises** *p.130*

vocabulary jobs

1 Match the words and pictures.

a <u>house</u>wife
an en<u>gi</u>neer
an <u>office</u> worker
a <u>wai</u>ter
a <u>law</u>yer
a po<u>lice</u> officer
a <u>busi</u>nessman / woman
a <u>shop</u> assistant
an <u>ac</u>tor
a <u>jour</u>nalist

2 **pronunciation** Listen. <u>Underline</u> the stress.
Listen again and practise.

3 With a partner, talk about the pictures.

examples **He's a** police officer. **She's a** shop assistant.

4 What do <u>you</u> do? (Use a dictionary if necessary.) Ask five people.

What do you do?

I'm a business student.
What do you do?

I'm an office worker.
And you?

grammar *a / an*

1 <u>Underline</u> the correct answer in the table.

a /ə/ / **an** /ən/
Put *a / an* before words that begin *a, e, i, o, u* e.g. <u>a</u>ctor, <u>e</u>ngineer
Put *a / an* before all other letters, e.g. <u>w</u>aiter, <u>t</u>eacher

2 Write *a* or *an.*

1 __ restaurant
2 __ taxi
3 __ airport
4 __ office worker

5 __ passport
6 __ e-mail
7 __ English book
8 __ job

go to **language reference** *and* **practice exercises** *p.130*

speaking it's your turn!

1 **Think!** Complete the sentences. Then tell a partner.

ME

My name's _____ .
I'm from _____ . (country / town)
I'm a / an _____ . (job)
I'm _____ . (married / single)

2 Tell two new students about yourself. Complete the table about the students.

	STUDENT 1	STUDENT 2
NAME	_____	_____
COUNTRY / TOWN	_____	_____
JOB	_____	_____
MARRIED / SINGLE	_____	_____

3 Find a new partner. Tell them about the two students.

That's Yoko. She's from
Japan, and she's ...

can you remember ...

... how to complete these sentences?

1 Hi, nice to _____ you.
2 I'm _____ France.
3 He's _____ engineer.
4 What do you _____ ?
5 I'm _____ (30).
6 She _____ married. (= She's single.)

wordbooster

countries and nationalities

1 For each country, write:

E (Europe)   A (Asia)   SA (South America)

COUNTRY	E? A? SA?	NATIONALITY
France	E	Fr __ nch
Germany		G __ rm __ n
Japan		J __ p __ n __ s __
Spain		Sp __ n __ sh
Argentina		__ rg __ nt __ n __ __ n
China		Ch __ n __ s __
Italy		__ t __ l __ __ n
Brazil		Br __ z __ l __ __ n
Thailand		Th __ __
Poland		P __ l __ sh
Britain		Br __ t __ sh
your country? _____		_____

> **Remember!**
> Countries and nationalities have capital letters: *France, French*

2  Listen and check. Practise saying the countries. Stress the underlined syllables.

3 Complete the nationalities with *a, e, i,* or *o*.

4 (1.6) pronunciation Listen. Underline the stressed syllable. Practise saying the nationalities.

5 Look at the pictures. Say the nationalities, like this:

He's / She's (French).   It's (= It is) ...   They're (= They are) ...
That's right ...   I'm not sure.   I don't know.

numbers (1)

1 (1.7) Listen. Complete the phone numbers.

Chris	042 69 _
Simone	31 _ 7 _ 8
Jane	37 _ 24 _
Kate	2 _ 5 99 _ _
Gerry	_ 84 _ _ 36
Charlotte	6 _ _ 5 _ _ 7

2 Work in A / B pairs. A – read a phone number, but change one number. B – correct it.

example **A** Chris – 043 694.
B No, it's 04<u>2</u> 694.

3 (1.8) natural English Listen. Which words in orange do you hear? Practise the dialogue.

> **natural English**
> *What's your phone number?*
>
> **A** What's your phone number / mobile number ?
> **B** It's 0779 242 1486.
> **A** 0779 242 1486?
> **B** Yeah / Yes, that's it.

4 Ask five people for their phone numbers. Write them down.

5 Complete these numbers with a partner.

a 3, 6, 9, __ , __ .

b 15, 25, 35, __ , __ .

c 7, 14, 21, __ , __ .

d 70, 80, 90, __ , __ .

e 60, 16, 50, 15, __ , __ .

f 5, 15, 45, __ , __ .

6 (1.9) Listen and check.

reading
questions, questions

can you remember ...

... eight countries and nationalities?
Tell a partner.

grammar questions with *be*

1   With a partner, complete column 1 with
    's (*is*) or *are*, and then complete column 2.

1	2	3	4
questions with *be*	question form	positive / negative	your answers
1 ___ you a new student?	___ you?	you are / aren't	
2 Where ___ you from?			
3 What level ___ your English?	___ he / she / it?	he / she / it is / isn't	
4 Who ___ your teacher?			
5 Where ___ she (or he) from?			
6 What ___ your room number?			
7 How many students ___ in the class?	___ they?	they are / aren't	
8 What nationality ___ they?			

2   (1.10)   Listen and check. Then think about your answers.

3   Complete column 4. If necessary, write *I don't know* or *I'm not sure*.

4   Work with a partner. Ask and answer the questions.

go to **language reference** *and* **practice exercises** *p.130*

read on

1 Read the e-mail. Tick ✓ the correct answer.

The e-mail is from Polly to her mother / Polly to Daniela.

The photo is of Juliet and Daniela / Polly and Daniela.

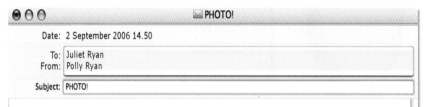

Date: 2 September 2006 14.50

To: Juliet Ryan
From: Polly Ryan

Subject: PHOTO!

Hi Mum

This is a photo of me and Daniela – she's in my class at drama college. She's from Argentina and she's very nice. She's over here with her boyfriend, Paolo, who's from Brazil. Her English is very good – she's advanced – she understands everything. We like the class very much. The teachers are fantastic ... and there are only eight students: me and Daniela, a boy from Poland, and all the others are British.

Yesterday, we ...

2 Order the questions about Daniela. Compare with a partner.

example 's / where / from / she?
Where's she from?

1 here / she / 's / why?

2 level / what / her English / 's?

3 are / in / how many / students / her class?

4 where / from / are / they?

5 's / her / who / boyfriend?

6 where / he / from / 's?

3 With your partner, ask and answer the questions.

4 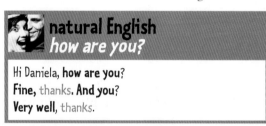 **natural English** Listen to Daniela and Polly in a bar. Do you hear the words in orange?

natural English
how are you?

Hi Daniela, **how are you?**
Fine, thanks. **And you?**
Very well, thanks.

5 pronunciation Listen again. What's the pronunciation of *How are you?* and *And you?*

6 Practise with a partner. Then practise with three more people.

vocabulary drinks

1 Match words from A and B, and with pictures 1 to 8.

example white wine = picture 3

white	coke
orange	chocolate
mineral	wine
black	juice
tea	wine
red	coffee
diet	water
hot	with lemon

2 (1.12) Listen and practise.

test your partner

– Wine?

– That's right.

– White wine.

3 (1.13) **natural English** Listen and complete the box.

4 **pronunciation** Listen again. What's the pronunciation of *would you*?

5 Practise the conversation with a partner. Ask for different drinks.

speaking it's your turn!

1 You meet a British friend in a café after your first English lesson. Work with a partner. Write the conversation.

your friend	you
ask *How are you?* 'Hi, João – how are you?'	answer
What level?	answer
How many students?	answer
nationality?	answer
teacher?	answer
ask *Would you like ...?*	answer
OK	answer

2 Practise with your partner. Change roles.

3 Practise with a new partner.

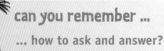

can you remember ...

... how to ask and answer?

1 **A** How _____ you?
   B _____ , thanks.
2 **A** _____ you like a drink?
   B Yes, _____ .
3 **A** _____ they British?
   B I'm _____ sure.

help with pronunciation and listening

Aa Bb Cc Dd Ee Ff Gg Hh Ii Jj Kk Ll Mm Nn Oo Pp Qq Rr Ss Tt Uu Vv Ww Xx Yy Zz

1 **(1.14)** Listen and practise the alphabet.

2 With a partner, practise the letters by colour:

A, H, ...   B, C, ...

3 **Cover the alphabet. Write the letters for these sounds.**

/eɪ/	/iː/	/e/
e.g. A	e.g. B	e.g. F

4 **Work in A / B pairs.**

A Ask B these questions and write the answers.

How do you spell:

– your first name?

– your family name?

– the name of your street?

B Answer the questions. Then change roles.

---

listening asking for help

Important!
When you listen, ask for help
if you don't understand.

1 natural English Match the questions with the pictures.

natural English
asking for help

Sorry, can you repeat that, please? Yes, sure.
Sorry, can you play that again, please? Yes, of course.

2 **(1.15)** Listen. What's the pronunciation of *can*?

3 pronunciation Listen again and practise the intonation.

4 **(1.16)** Susannah wants to study at Oxford Community College. Listen and complete the form.

OXFORD COMMUNITY COLLEGE

name _____

nationality _____

age _____

address _____

postcode _____

phone number _____

5 **Compare with a partner. Ask your teacher to play it again if necessary.**

Susannah

one review

vocabulary countries and nationalities

Write five countries and five nationalities using the letters.

examples FRance   CHinese

JA SP
FR CH AR
BR
PO TH GE
IT

grammar *be*

test your partner
– France
– That's a country.
– That's right.

Order the words, and add the correct form of *be*.

	+ *be*	sentence
example teacher / your / America / from?	*is*	Is your teacher from America?
1 your / people / many / class / how / in?	___	_____
2 you / student / new / a?	___	_____
3 David / married / Catherine / to?	___	_____
4 I / from / not / Germany	___	_____
5 the / room two / class / not / in	___	_____
6 phone / what / your / number?	___	_____

natural English

1 Write <u>one</u> word in each gap. Compare with a partner.

   1 A Hello. I'm Mark.
      B Hi. _____ to meet you. I'm Clare.
   2 A Hi. How are you?
      B _____, thanks. And you?
      A I'm very _____, thanks.
   3 A _____ you like a drink?
      B Oh, yes, please.
   4 A Look at page 84.
      B Sorry, _____ you repeat that, _____?
      A Yes, _____. Page 84.

2 Check your answers using the **natural English** boxes in unit one.
   Practise the dialogues with your partner.

numbers and the alphabet

go to **pairwork** *on p.119*

---

test yourself!

Now cover the REVIEW section and test yourself on unit one.

test your vocabulary

From this unit, write down:

1 six more jobs: *teacher, doctor, ...*
2 the nationality of these countries: *Britain, Japan, Spain, Poland, Brazil, France*
3 words to complete these drinks:
   black _____
   mineral _____
   orange _____
   red _____

score | 16 |

gap-fill

Fill the gaps.

1 My name's Caroline. Nice to _____ you.
2 She _____ married – she's single.
3 A _____ are you?
   B _____, thanks. And you?
4 A _____ you like a drink?
   B Yes, please.

score | 5 |

error correction

Correct the errors.

1 I'm engineer.
2 What's your number phone?
3 I not sure.
4 A He is a teacher?
   B Yes, he is.

score | 4 |

total score | 25 |

Look back at the unit contents on *p.6*. Tick ✓ the language you can use.

things

tick ✓ when you know this

natural English
- [ ] *thing(s)*
- [ ] giving opinions (1)
- [ ] *Can I ...? / Can you ...?*
- [ ] saying you aren't sure

grammar
- [ ] *have got (= have)*
- [ ] possessive *'s*
- [ ] *this, that, these, those*

vocabulary
- [ ] technology
- [ ] personal things
- [ ] adjectives (1)

reading
have you got one?

vocabulary technology

1 Match the words to the pictures.

TV	mobile (phone)	DVD player	printer
computer	digital camera	CD player	laptop

2 **pronunciation** Practise the words. Stress the <u>underlined</u> syllable.

15

read on

1 Look at the advert. Answer the questions.

1 What's the name of the shop?
2 How much is the laptop normally?
3 How much is it this weekend?
4 Is there a free printer with the laptop?
5 Is the Entel a colour printer?
6 Which two things take photos?
7 How big is the TV screen?
8 Which two things have stereo sound?

Tell a partner your answers.

2 Listen. Write this weekend's prices in the **red** boxes in the advert.

3 **natural English.** Read the box. Write *thing* or *things*.

thing(s)

What's this _____ ?
It's a DVD player.
How many _____ are in the advert?
Eight.
This _____'s fantastic.

4 Listen and check. How do you say *thing* in your language?

www.thetechshop.com

THE TECH SHOP
special prices this weekend!

SYNTAC COMPUTER
40cm monitor
perfect for work, study, Internet use
normal price €750   this weekend €680

CIBA LAPTOP
38cm monitor
use the Internet and e-mail when you want
normally €875   this weekend €800   info

ENTEL PRINTER
fast, excellent quality
16 pages a minute in black and white
12 pages a minute in colour
normal price €190   this weekend €____   info

SONIC DIGITAL CAMERA
great photos and easy to use
X5 zoom
normal price €130   this weekend €____

eTONE MOBILE PHONE
includes games and digital camera
normally €125   this weekend €____

SASSO PERSONAL CD PLAYER
15 hours playing time
super stereo sound
normal price €40   this weekend €____

RJC WIDESCREEN TV
66 cm screen
stereo sound
normally €555   this weekend €____

EITO DVD PLAYER
super digital picture
remote control
normal price €90   this weekend €____

grammar *have got* (= *have*)

1 Read the dialogue. <u>Underline</u> examples of *have got*.

A <u>Have you got</u> these things?

B Which things?

A The things in the photos.

B I've got a TV – it's in my bedroom – and I've also got a computer and printer.

A What about a laptop?

B No, I haven't got a laptop, and I haven't got a digital camera.

2 Tell a partner the things *you've got* and the things *you haven't got*:

I've got a computer.

I haven't got a laptop.

3 **Think!** Write five sentences about your family. Tell a partner.

In my family, we've got three TVs.

My father's got a digital camera, and he's got a computer.

My mother's got a computer too, and she's got a mobile.

4 Complete the table.

positive		negative	
I' ____ *got*		I ____ *got*	
He / She' ____ ____	} a TV.	He / She ____ ____	} a printer.
We / They' ____ ____		We / They ____ ____	

question form		short answers
____ you *got*		Yes, I have. / No, I haven't.
____ he / she ____	} a camera?	Yes, he has. / No, he hasn't.
____ we / they ____		Yes, we have. / No, we haven't.

5 Complete the conversations.

A ¹ _____ you got a mobile phone?

B Yes, I ² _____ .

A What make is it?

B It' ³ _____ a Nokia.

A Are you happy with it?

B Yes, ⁴ _____ 's fine.

C ⁵ _____ your brother got a computer?

D Yes, he ⁶ _____ .

C ⁷ _____ it good?

D Yes, it' ⁸ _____ fantastic.

C Oh, really? What make is ⁹ _____ ?

D I think he' ¹⁰ _____ got an Apple Mac.

6 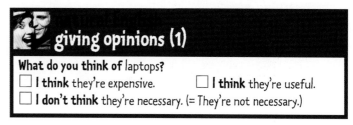 Listen and check. Practise with a partner.

7 Speak to four different people in the same way:

Have you got a ...?   What make is it?

Are you happy with it?

go to **language reference** *and* **practice exercises** *p.131*

speaking   it's your turn!

1 natural English Listen and number the answers in order (**1, 2, 3**).

giving opinions (1)

What do you think of laptops?

☐ **I think** they're expensive.   ☐ **I think** they're useful.

☐ **I don't think** they're necessary. (= They're not necessary.)

2 Practise saying the sentences.

3 **Think!** What do <u>you</u> think of the things in the advert? Ask other people. Use the **natural English** phrases.

What do you think of DVD players?

I think they're ...

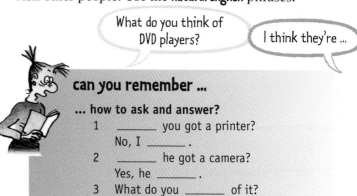

can you remember ...

... how to ask and answer?

1 _____ you got a printer?
   No, I _____ .

2 _____ he got a camera?
   Yes, he _____ .

3 What do you _____ of it?
   I _____ it's expensive.

wordbooster

personal things

1 Match the words to the things in the picture.

pencil	notebook	dictionary	briefcase	magazine
bag	travel card	piece of paper	coursebook	lighter
rubber	newspaper	pen	keys	

Paula Christophe

2  **pronunciation Listen and practise the word stress.**

3 What has your partner got? Tell him / her. Guess if you don't know.

examples   **You've got** a notebook and a pen.
I think you've got a dictionary.
You haven't got a lighter.

possessive 's

1 Think about the answers.

1 Where's Paula**'s** pen? (NOT ~~the pen of Paula~~)
2 Is Christophe**'s** briefcase new? (NOT ~~the briefcase of Christophe~~)
3 Is Paula**'s** magazine English or Spanish?
4 What colour is Christophe**'s** lighter?

2 Ask and answer with a partner. Remember the 's.

3 Play the memory game. Go to *p.119.*

adjectives (1)

1 Find opposites from the two circles.
example   hot and cold

cheap
noisy great
interesting
difficult similar
safe
~~hot~~ early
dark

different
~~cold~~ quiet
late
terrible boring
light
expensive easy
dangerous

2  **Listen and check.**

test your partner
– What's the opposite of 'cheap'?
– Expensive.
– That's right.

3 Do you know these colours? Complete the words.

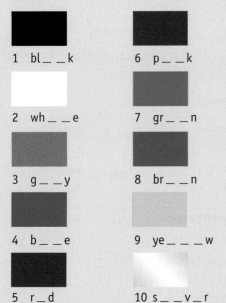

1 bl _ _ k
2 wh _ _ e
3 g _ _ y
4 b _ _ e
5 r _ d

6 p _ _ k
7 gr _ _ n
8 br _ _ n
9 ye _ _ _ w
10 s _ _ v _ r

listening
how to ... ask for things

lead-in

1 **natural English** Listen. Match the questions with the answers. (2.7)

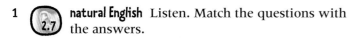

Can I ...? | Can you ...?

Can I look at your newspaper, please?	Yes, **sure.**
Can I borrow* your rubber, please?	Yes, **here you are.**
Can you open the window, please?	Yes, **of course.**

* **borrow** (v) have for a short time, then give back

2 **pronunciation** Listen and practise the conversations with a partner. Stress the underlined syllables.

3 Complete the questions using the pictures. Then practise with a partner.

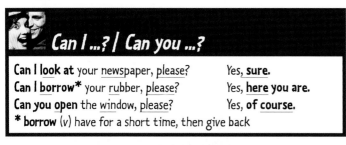

1 A It's hot in here. Can you turn on the _____ ?
   B Yes, of course.
2 A It's noisy. Can you close the _____ ?
   B Sure.
3 A It's hot in here. Can you turn off the _____ ?
   B Yeah, sure.
4 A It's dark in here. Can you turn on the _____ ?
   B Yeah.

4 With your partner, have more conversations. Use these words.

   hot cold dark noisy open / close turn on / turn off

grammar *this, that, these, those*

1 (2.8) Listen. Underline the correct word.

Is this / that your dictionary?

Is this / that your bag?

Are these / those keys Bruno's?

Are these / those books Julia's?

2 **pronunciation** Listen again. What's the pronunciation of *this, that, these,* and *those?*

3 Go to the tapescript on *p.147*. Practise the conversations with a partner.

4 Complete the table with *this*, *that*, *these*, or *those*.

	singular	plural
near me	_____ pen	_____ pens
not near me	_____ phone	_____ phones

5 Look at the pictures in **exercise 1** on *p.19*. Practise similar conversations, but this time talk about:

picture 1 the rubber   picture 3 the lighter
picture 2 the books   picture 4 the magazine

6 With a partner, walk round the class and talk about things on the tables.

examples I think that's Dagmar's pen.
            Those are Franco's books.

go to language reference *and* practice exercises *p.132*

listen to this

tune in

1 **(2.9)** Listen. Which sentence do you hear?

1 I haven't got a book.   I haven't got my book.
2 What page is it?   OR   What unit is it?
3 I've got a pen.   I haven't got a pen.

listen carefully

2 **(2.10)** It's the beginning of a lesson. Listen to the teacher and answer the questions.

1 What country is the lesson about?
2 What's the teacher's question?
3 Is David's answer correct?
4 What page is it in the book?

listening challenge

3 **(2.11)** Listen. It's the end of the lesson. What's the homework?

listen again with the tapescript *p.147*

4 **(2.12)** natural English. Read the box, then listen. Do you hear the *t* in *can't* and *don't* ?

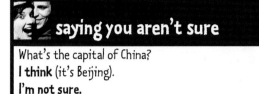

saying you aren't sure

What's the capital of China?
I think (it's Beijing).
I'm not sure.
I can't remember.
I don't know.

Practise the phrases.

5 Work in A / B pairs. Use the **natural English** phrases.

A – go to *p.119*.   B – go to *p.120*.

writing

1 Look at the notes. With a partner, correct:

1 eight mistakes with capital letters, e.g. Thailand, NOT ~~thailand~~

2 six punctuation mistakes e.g. I'm NOT ~~Im~~

andré
ive got some difficult french
homework this weekend. can
I borrow your french / english
dictionary, please
            Thanks,
        caroline

Olga

whats the school
phone number. i cant
remember

Yuri

2 Write a note to your partner in the same way. Begin:

Can I ...? or *Can you ...?* or *What's ...?*

3 Read your partner's note and write an answer.

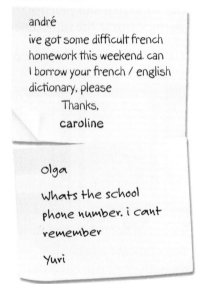

can you remember ...

... the plural of *this* and the plural of *that*?

help with pronunciation and listening

pronunciation word stress

1 (2.13) **Listen and repeat the words in the table. The stress is <u>underlined</u>.**

Oo	oO	Ooo	oOo	ooO
<u>lis</u>ten	re<u>peat</u>	<u>It</u>aly	re<u>mem</u>ber	engi<u>neer</u>

2 **Write these words in the table above.**

complete	understand
English	pronounce
expensive	difficult
computer	answer
practise	Japanese
interesting	question

3 (2.14) **Listen and repeat the sentences.**

Listen and repeat.

It's difficult to pronounce 'interesting'.

How do you spell 'Japanese'?

Can you complete the sentence?

Remember to practise your English.

I don't understand the question.

listening information words

Important!
When you listen, information words are LOUDER. They help you understand the speaker.

1 Read *WHAT IS IT?* Tell a partner the answer.

WHAT IS IT?

Well, I've got one at home. I need it for <u>work</u> and for my <u>studies</u> too. It's quite <u>small</u> – I can put it in my <u>briefcase</u> – and it's <u>white</u>.

It was very expensive, but I use it every day. I can write letters on it and send e-mails and I can look up things on the Internet.

2 (2.15) **Listen and read. <u>Underline</u> important information words in the second paragraph.**

3 (2.16) **Listen to the woman. Tick ✓ the words you hear.**

☐	at home	☐	turn it on
☐	at work	☐	turn it off
☐	big	☐	watch
☐	small	☐	listen
☐	black	☐	morning
☐	white	☐	evening

4 **What is she talking about?**

listen again with the **tapescript** *p.147*

two review

vocabulary personal things

go to **pairwork** *p.119*

vocabulary adjectives (1)

1 Work in A / B pairs. B – go to *p.120*.

A – write the opposites.

cheap noisy difficult safe hot early interesting great

2 Check with your partner.

3 Work with your partner. Which adjectives from **exercise 1** go before these nouns?

film water exercise street watch book party train

grammar questions and answers

1 (R2.1) Listen. Number the pictures in the correct order.

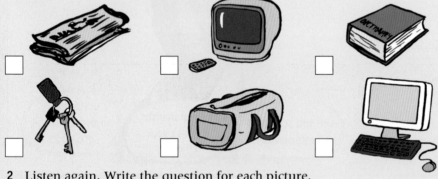

2 Listen again. Write the question for each picture.

1 _____ ?   4 _____ ?
2 _____ ?   5 _____ ?
3 _____ ?   6 _____ ?

3 With your partner, can you remember the answers to the questions?

natural English

1 Put the pink words in the correct place.

can't

example	I ʌremember.	CAN'T
1	Can I borrow lighter, please?	YOUR
2	Yes, sure. Here are.	YOU
3	What's this in English?	THING
4	I'm sure.	NOT
5	I think TV is very important.	DON'T
6	I look at your newspaper, please?	CAN

2 Check your answers using the **natural English** boxes in unit two.

---

test yourself!

Now cover the REVIEW section and test yourself on unit two.

test your vocabulary
From this unit:

1 write five more things like this:
   DVD player, digital camera, ...
2 complete these personal things:
   r_ bb _ r
   n _ wsp _ p _ r
   d _ ct _ _ n _ ry
   br _ _ fc _ s _
   l _ ght _ r
   tr _ v _ l c _ rd
   n _ t _ b _ _ k
3 write the opposites,
   e.g. *boring – interesting*:
   difficult, safe, early, quiet, expensive

   score [17]

gap-fill
Fill the gaps.

1 A Can I _____ your pen for a minute, please?
   B Sure.
2 A Can I look at your newspaper, please?
   B Yes, _____ you are.
3 Has your teacher _____ a car?
4 I've got a piece of paper, but I _____ got a pen.

   score [4]

error correction
Correct the errors.

1 I not think it's necessary.
2 Is this David book?
3 A What's the capital of Peru?
   B I not remember.
4 Are this your keys?

   score [4]

   total score [25]

Look back at the unit contents on *p.15*. Tick ✓ the language you can use.

---

listening
you and me

vocabulary noun groups

1 Work with a partner. Find words that go together in columns 1, 2, and 3.

example Towns and villages are places where we live.

1	2	3
towns	trains	things we eat
basketball	factories	games
coffee	villages	places where we work
buses	bread	places where we live
offices	beer	forms of transport
rice	flats	types of home
houses	tennis	types of drink

and ... are

2 (3.1) Listen and check.

3 **pronunciation** Listen again. What's the pronunciation of:

villages places buses offices factories houses?

test your partner

– Places where we live?
– Yes.
– Towns and villages.

grammar present simple

1 Tick ✓ the sentences in the table below that are true for you.

	you	your partner	Jonathan
HOMES			
I live in a town.			
I live in a village.			
I live in a house.			
I live in a flat.			
WORK / STUDY			
I work in an office.			
I work in a factory.			
I work at home.			
I study English at university.			
I study English at a language school.			
TRANSPORT			
I drive to work / school / university.			
I walk to work / school / university.			
I take the bus / train.			
FREE TIME			
I stay at home a lot.			
I go out a lot.			
I play basketball.			
I play tennis.			
I listen to music a lot.			
FOOD AND DRINK			
I drink a lot of coffee.			
I eat a lot of rice.			

2 Read your true sentences to a partner. Then complete the 'your partner' column.

3 Listen to Jonathan. Tick ✓ the sentences that are true for him. Listen again if necessary.

4  **natural English** Listen and complete. Then practise the sentences.

> **natural English**
> **a lot (of)** /ə'lɒtəv/
>
> I play _____ **a lot**.
> NOT ~~I play tennis a lot of.~~
> I drink **a lot of** _____.

5 Look at the sentences below. Then say the sentences in the table that are <u>not</u> true for you.

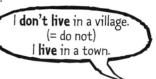

> I **don't live** in a village.
> (= do not)
> I **live** in a town.

6  **pronunciation** Listen. What's the pronunciation of *do you*?

> **Do you play** tennis?
> Yes, I do.
>
> **Do you study** English at university?
> No, I don't.

Practise the dialogues.

7 Complete the table.

PRESENT SIMPLE	
positive	**negative**
I / You **speak** Spanish.	I __ __ Japanese.
We / They **live** in a town.	We __ __ in a village.
questions	**short answers**
__ you __ English?	Yes, I __ .
__ they __ in a flat?	No, they __ .

go to **language reference** *and* **practice exercises** *p.132*

8 Find a <u>new</u> partner. Ask and answer questions from the table in **exercise 1**.

listen to this

tune in

1 **⟨3.5⟩** Wendy Bolton is from Bath City Transport. She telephones Mr Roberts to ask him some questions. Listen to the first part of the conversation and complete the address on the form.

Hello?

Oh, good morning. Is that Mr Roberts?

NAME	Andrew Roberts
HOME ADDRESS	_____ Kipling Avenue, Bath, _____ 4PH
JOB	history _____
WORK ADDRESS	King Edward _____ , North Road
TRANSPORT	_____
REASON	buses are terrible
DISTANCE	_____ miles (1 mile = 1.6 kilometres)
LEAVE HOME AT	_____
GET TO WORK AT	_____

listen carefully

2 Listen to the whole conversation and complete the form.

listening challenge

3 **⟨3.6⟩** Listen. Does Mr Roberts drive at the weekend? If yes, where?

listen again with the **tapescript** *p.148*

4 **natural English** Find a question from the box in tapescript 3.5.

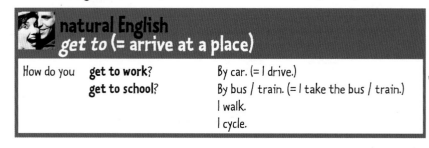

natural English
get to (= arrive at a place)

How do you	**get to work?**	By car. (= I drive.)
	get to school?	By bus / train. (= I take the bus / train.)
		I walk.
		I cycle.

5 Stand up. Ask five people the questions.

grammar *wh-* questions

1 Complete the questions with these words.

Where   How   Why   How far   What   When (x2)

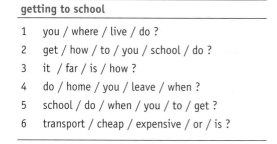

1	*What's* your name?	*Marsha Van Praag*
2	_____ 's your address?	*26 Elton Road*
3	_____ do you work?	*National Bank of Ireland*
4	_____ do you get to work?	*by bus*
5	_____ is it to your office?	*two miles*
6	_____ do you leave home?	*8.00*
7	_____ do you get to work?	*8.30*
8	_____ do you go by bus?	*it's cheap*

2 Practise the questions and answers with a partner.

go to **language reference** *and* **practice exercises** *p.133*

3 Order the words to make questions.

getting to school

1 you / where / live / do ?
2 get / how / to / you / school / do ?
3 it / far / is / how ?
4 do / home / you / leave / when ?
5 school / do / when / you / to / get ?
6 transport / cheap / expensive / or / is ?

speaking it's your turn!

1 **Think!** Answer the questions in **exercise 3**.

2 Stand up and ask three people.

Where do you live?

I live in ...

can you remember ...

... verbs that go in these sentences?
I _____ in a flat.
I _____ in a bank.
Do you _____ the train to work?
I _____ to work at 8.15.
I don't _____ to music a lot.
I _____ to the cinema a lot.

wordbooster

telling the time

1 Complete the times.

three o'_____

_____ past four

five fifteen OR
_____ past five

six thirty OR _____
past six

_____ to eight

eight forty-five OR
_____ to nine

2 (3.7) Listen and check. Practise the times.

3 (3.8) **natural English** Listen and complete the question in the box.

4 Work with a partner. Cover the words in **exercise 1**. Ask and answer using the clocks and the natural English phrases.

5 A – go to *p.120*. B – go to *p.122*.

leisure activities

1 Match the words and pictures.

| swimming | skiing | cooking | | shopping | driving |
| dancing | travelling | going to the gym | | sightseeing | computer games |

1

2

3

4

5

6

7

8

9

10

2 (3.9) **pronunciation** Listen and repeat. Stress the <u>underlined</u> syllables.

test your partner
– What's this?
– Skiing.
– That's right.

reading
how to ... talk about likes and dislikes

lead-in

1 🔊 **natural English.** Listen and complete. Then practise the
3.10 sentences.

> **natural English**
> **likes and dislikes**
>
> After *like / hate*, use a noun or *-ing* form.
>
> 🙂 I really like _____.   🙂 I quite like _____.
>
> ☹ I don't like _____.   ☹ I hate _____.

2 In small groups, talk about the activities on *p.26* using the **natural English** phrases.

   examples I quite like swimming.   I don't like going to the gym.

   go to **language reference** *and* **practice exercises** *p.133*

grammar present simple with *he / she*

1 Look at the sentences below. Why do we say *likes / doesn't like*, and not *like / don't like*?

   Marco **likes** travelling.   He **doesn't like** pop music.

2 With a partner, complete the sentences in the table. If you don't know, guess.

   examples He speaks Spanish. (speak)

   She doesn't understand Japanese. (understand)

> **What do you know about your teacher?**
> _____ Spanish. (speak)
> _____ Japanese. (understand)
> _____ chocolate. (like)
> _____ dancing. (like)
> _____ in a flat. (live)
> _____ at home. (work)
> _____ on Saturdays. (work)
> _____ beer. (drink)
> _____ to the cinema a lot. (go)

3 Tell another pair your answers.

   example (We think) she speaks Spanish.

4 Ask your teacher for the answers. How many of your sentences are true?

5 Complete the table with the verb *speak*.

PRESENT SIMPLE *HE / SHE / IT*	
positive	negative
He / She ___ Thai.	He / She ___ ___ Thai.
questions	short answers
___ he / she ___ Thai?	Yes, he / she ___.
	No, he / she ___.

6 Ask your partner questions about other students, using the table in **exercise 2**.

   example A Does Marcel speak Spanish?
              B No, he doesn't. / I don't know.

   go to **language reference** *and* **practice exercises** *p.133*

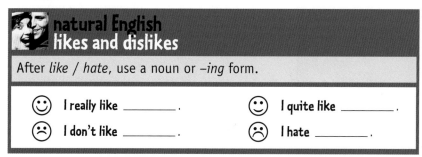

read on

1 Read the introduction. Write the numbers in sentences a to c.

   2   17   29

a _____ people work for 'La Strada'.

b _____ people at 'La Strada' are British.

c There are _____ different nationalities.

2 Read about the workers. Who <u>doesn't</u> like the job?

Workers of the world

Britain is the workshop of the world. In just one business in the centre of London – the group of sandwich bars 'La Strada' – only two workers out of twenty-nine are British. The other twenty-seven workers come from sixteen different countries, including Spain, South Korea, Turkey, and Jamaica.

BELÉN AVILA from Spain
I work here in the afternoon and evening, but in the morning I go to English lessons. The café is fantastic and I've got a lot of friends here, but London is very expensive.

SANG MIN from South Korea
I'm a barista (coffee maker) here. I've got a small flat in London with two friends from work. London's a great city to live in and the job's very good, but I want to go to Japan to work next year.

ALİ DEMİR from Turkey
I'm married to an English woman and we want to buy a house together. I'm a manager now and I really like my job, but I don't like working long hours. London is very **cosmopolitan** and an interesting place to live.

SUZETTE LANGLAND from Jamaica
I've got family in London, so I live with them. I want to study business administration here and live in London **permanently**. The people are friendly, but the job is boring. And I hate the **rain**!

3 Complete the sentences using the present simple.

1 Suzette _____ with her family.

2 Sang Min _____ coffee at La Strada.

3 Belén _____ at La Strada in the morning.

4 Sang Min _____ to go to Asia.

5 Ali _____ working long hours.

6 Suzette _____ to study business.

7 Belén _____ English in the morning.

8 Ali _____ to buy a house.

Read the sentences to a partner.

4 Complete the time expressions with <u>one</u> word. Check your answers in the article.

__ the morning   __ the afternoon
__ the evening

speaking it's your turn!

1 **Think!** Do you know anyone who works in another city or country?

   Who is it?
   Where does he / she work?
   What does he / she do?
   Does he / she like it?
   Why / Why not?

2 Stand up. Ask three people about their person.

> Have you got a friend who works in another city?

> Yes, my friend Paco lives in ...

can you remember ...

... the verbs that go in these sentences?

_____ you like New York?

_____ your teacher speak Italian?

He really _____ travelling.

She _____ speak German.

glossary

cosmopolitan (adj) /ˌkɒzməˈpɒlɪtən/ with people from many different countries

permanently (adv) /ˈpɜːmənəntli/ for a long time

rain (n) /reɪn/

extended speaking
how active are you?

you're going to:

collect ideas	listen	do an interview	write a paragraph
complete a leisure activities questionnaire	listen to people talking about the questionnaire	interview a partner	write about your partner

 ## collect ideas

1 With a partner, fill the gaps in the table. Use the pictures to help you.

2 **Think!** Tick ✓ 'yes' or 'no' in the 'you' column and complete part 4 of the table. Use a dictionary if necessary.

3 Ask and answer the questions with a partner.

 ## listen

4 (3.11) Listen. Which three things in the questionnaire do Nick and Lynne talk about?

5 Listen again. Write down Nick's questions. What are Lynne's answers?

 ## interview

6 **Think!** Find a new partner. Look at his / her questionnaire. Think of <u>one</u> question for each 'yes' answer using these words.

What ...?   When ...?   Where ...?   Why ...?
How ...?   How far ...?

example   What do you watch on TV?

7 Interview your partner. Then look at the questionnaires together. Are you very active?

 ## writing

8 Read this paragraph.

> <u>My partner</u> (at home)
> Katrina stays at home and watches TV a lot. She watches the news and a lot of films. She listens to music (she really likes classical music), but she doesn't like computer games. She's not a very active person.

9 Write about your partner. Use one part of the questionnaire ('at home', 'outside', or 'sport').

Are you an active person?

		You		Your partner	
1 at home	Do you ...	yes	no	yes	no
	... stay at home a lot?				
	... _____ _____ a lot?				
	... play computer games a lot?				
	... _____ _____ a lot?				
2 outside	Do you ...				
	... go to the cinema a lot?				
	... go _____ a lot?				
	... go out and watch sport?				
	... _____ a lot?				
3 sport	Do you ...				
	... play football or rugby?				
	... _____ _____ or volleyball?				
	... go to the gym a lot?				
	... go _____ a lot?				

4 **What other things do you do?**
at home   _____
outside   _____
sport   _____

three review

grammar present simple

1 Write <u>one</u> word / contraction in each gap. Then compare with a partner.

¹ I'_____ got some old friends called Luis and Silvia. Luis ² _____ Brazilian and Silvia ³ _____ Mexican, but she ⁴ _____ Portuguese very well. ⁵ They'_____ married and they ⁶ _____ in Rio de Janeiro. Luis ⁷ _____ for an international bank. He ⁸ _____ to go to America next year to work. Silvia ⁹ _____ want to go because she really ¹⁰ _____ their beautiful flat in the Leblon area of Rio.

2 **Think!** Think about a friend who lives in a different town.

Who is he / she?   Where does he / she live?   Is he / she married?

What does he / she do?   What does he / she want to do in the future?

Write about your friend. Use the text above to help you.

vocabulary noun groups and leisure activities

1 <u>Underline</u> the one that is different in each group.

example	swimming	skiing	<u>shopping</u>	golf	(shopping isn't a sport)
a	bread	water	rice	chocolate
b	transport	bus	train	car
c	coffee	wine	flat	water
d	town	office	village	city
e	house	office	factory	shop
f	basketball	tennis	dancing	volleyball

2 Compare with a partner. Give reasons for your answers.

natural English

1 Order the words.

1 drink / a / I / of / coffee / lot

2 pop / really / I / music / like

3 likes / jazz / she / quite

4 the / excuse / have / time / me / got / you ?

5 past / it's / seven / quarter

6 he / to / get / how / school / does ?

2 Check your answers using the **natural English** boxes in unit three.

vocabulary telling the time

go to **pairwork** *p.123*

go to **pairwork** *p.123*

---

tick ✓ when you know this

natural English
- [ ] *about an hour a day / week*
- [ ] asking about family
- [ ] *(do something) together*
- [ ] saying thank you

grammar
- [ ] present simple with frequency adverbs
- [ ] possessive adjectives: *my, your,* etc.

vocabulary
- [ ] daily routines
- [ ] days, months, and seasons
- [ ] time phrases with prepositions
- [ ] families

reading
habits

vocabulary daily routines

1 Look at the table. Number the phrases in a logical order.

2 🔊 **4.1** Listen to Holly. Is her order the same?

3 Listen again. Write the time for <u>six</u> things that she does in the 'HOLLY when?' column.

4 Tell a partner about Holly's day.

example   She gets up at six-thirty and then she …

	order?	HOLLY when?	YOU when? e.g. 7.30	how often? *always, usually,* etc.
have lunch				
watch TV				
get up	1			
read the paper				
have dinner				
leave home				
go to bed				
get to school / university / work				
have breakfast				
get home				

Holly

grammar present simple with frequency adverbs

1 Find these words in tapescript 4.1 on *p.148*. Put them in the table below.

never   ~~always~~   usually / often   hardly ever   sometimes

100% always				0%
	_____	_____	_____	_____

2 Look at the sentences. Circle the correct word in the rule.

always		sometimes

I **am** late for school.   I **read** the newspaper in the morning.

Put *always, sometimes, never,* etc. before / after the verb *be*.

Put *always, sometimes, never,* etc. before / after most other verbs.

3 Put the adverbs in the correct place. Check with tapescript 4.1 on *p.148*.

1 I get up at 6.30. ALWAYS
2 I go out. HARDLY EVER
3 I am in bed before eleven. ALWAYS
4 I have lunch at 1.00. USUALLY
5 I read the paper. OFTEN
6 I'm tired in the evening. ALWAYS

go to **language reference** *and* **practice exercises** *p.134*

4 **Think!** Complete the 'YOU when?' and the 'YOU how often?' columns in **vocabulary exercise 1** on *p.31*.

5 Find a new partner. Tell them about your day.

example

I usually get up at ...

read on

1 Ask and answer in small groups.

1 Do you like reading?
2 What do you read? (newspapers? magazines? school / university books? novels? other?)

2 Read the first part of the article (*Who reads most?*). Complete table 1.

3 Read the rest of the article (*Where do people read?*). Write a phrase from the article or the table under each picture.

4 Read the article again. Are these sentences TRUE or FALSE?

1 People often read in bed.
2 Teachers don't read a lot in bed.
3 Accountants do 16% of their reading in the living room.
4 Taxi drivers don't read on the way to work.
5 People don't usually read in the bath.

Who reads most?

A **survey** of 1,600 people shows that **accountants** read more than people in other jobs – five hours and fifteen minutes a week. The survey asked people about reading in their free time, and some of the facts are quite surprising. In second place are **secretaries** with four hours and fifty-nine minutes a week. Bottom of the list are **priests** with only two hours and forty minutes. One told us that priests don't often read **for pleasure** because they are very busy people and don't have much free time.

TABLE 1 Who reads most?

Jobs	Hours a week
_____	5hrs 15
_____	4hrs 59
taxi drivers	4hrs 46
lawyers	4hrs 33
	2hrs 40

glossary

survey (n) questions you ask a lot of people
accountant (n) person who keeps a record of the money in a company
secretary (n) /ˈsekrətri/ person who works in an office, typing letters, answering the phone, etc.
priest (n) /priːst/

(read) for pleasure (read) because you like it
on the way (to work) travelling (to work)

Where do people read?

The place where most people read is in bed – teachers do 50% of their reading in bed. Accountants often read **on the way to work** (26% of their reading). Taxi drivers never read on the way to work (because they are driving), but they read a lot in their work breaks because they often sit in their taxis when they are not driving. Lawyers often read on holiday, when they can relax, but people hardly ever read in the bath.

TABLE 2 Where do people read?

	accountants	taxi drivers	lawyers	teachers
In bed	35%	24%	37%	50%
On holiday	15%	12%	37%	28%
In the living room	14%	10%	11%	14%
On the way to work	26%	0%	11%	1%
Work breaks	1%	50%	0%	0%
In the bathroom	3%	2%	0%	3%
Other	4%	2%	4%	4%

5 **natural English** Complete the sentences with one word. Check your answer in the article *Who reads most?*.

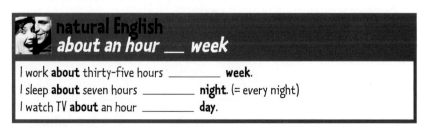

natural English
about an hour ___ week

I work **about** thirty-five hours _____ **week**.
I sleep **about** seven hours _____ **night**. (= every night)
I watch TV **about** an hour _____ **day**.

6   Listen and practise the sentences. Tell two people how many hours you sleep / watch TV / work / study.

speaking it's your turn!

1 **Think!** Read the tables below. Then write <u>true</u> sentences for you. Add your own ideas.

WHAT?

I always		a daily newspaper.
I often	**read**	magazines.
I sometimes	**buy**	books for school / university.
I hardly ever		books for pleasure.
I never		*your ideas*

WHERE?

I always		in bed.
I often		on holiday.
I sometimes	**read**	in the living room.
I hardly ever		in the bathroom.
I never		*your ideas*

HOW LONG?

I read	about five or ten minutes a day.
	about .... .

2 Ask and answer in small groups.

Mariko, what do you read?

Well, I read a lot of books for university, and I always read ...

Who reads most in your group?

can you remember ...

... the prepositions in these phrases?
he's ___ bed
she's ___ holiday
he's ___ the bathroom
she's ___ her way to work
he's ___ the living room
Check your answers in the article.

wordbooster

days, months, and seasons

1 Work with a partner. You have two minutes. Put the words below in order (1, 2, 3, etc.) and write the missing word.

_____ April
June February September
January 1
May November October
July March December

Monday Tuesday Sunday
Wednesday Saturday
Thursday

summer spring
autumn
_____

Remember!
Days and months begin with capital letters: Monday, January, etc.

2 pronunciation **Listen and say the next word.**

example October, November, …

December!

3 Play the game with a partner. Say two words, your partner says the next word.

time phrases with prepositions

1 Complete the time phrases in bold with words from the box.

| on | weekend | between | in | on | week | moment | at | winter |

1 I usually go out _____ **Thursday.**
2 He always gets here _____ **4 o'clock.**
3 My course starts _____ **September.**
4 We usually have a holiday _____ **May 1st.**
5 I always go skiing **in the** _____ .
6 We sometimes work **at the** _____ . (= on Saturday / Sunday)
7 I get up early **during the** _____ . (= from Monday to Friday)
8 She's on holiday **at the** _____ . (= now)
9 They have dinner _____ **7.30 and 8.00.**

2 Complete the rules about prepositions of time.

PREPOSITIONS OF TIME		
___ (a time)	___ (a day)	___ (a period)
examples		
___ three o'clock	___ Friday	___ August
___ 5.30	___ July 21st	___ the summer

3 Cover exercises 1 and 2. Complete these phrases.

___ the weekend	___ April	___ Monday
___ the week	___ 6.00 and 7.00	___ 11 o'clock
___ the spring	___ January 2nd	___ the moment

4 Work alone. Write your answers.

1 When do people in your country usually go on holiday?
2 What season do they go skiing?
3 When do they play football?
4 In which months is it very hot?
5 When is it cold?
6 Which days do people usually work?
7 Which day(s) are the shops closed?
8 Which day(s) do you have English classes?

Compare your answers in small groups.

listening

how to ... talk about your family

vocabulary families

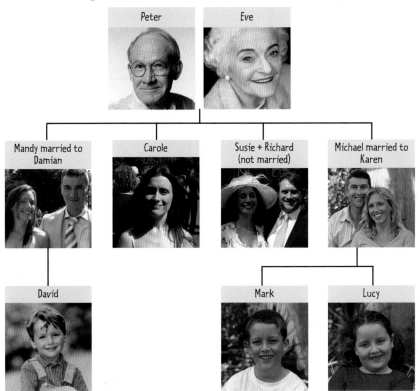

Peter   Eve

Mandy married to Damian   Carole   Susie + Richard (not married)   Michael married to Karen

David   Mark   Lucy

1 Complete the sentences with words from the box.

~~father~~	sister	niece	husband	girlfriend
daughter	~~son~~	aunt	children	nephew
uncle	wife	parents	mother	grandson
cousins	brother	boyfriend	grandmother	

1 Peter and Michael are _father_ and _son_.
2 Michael and Carole are _____ and _____ .
3 Susie and Richard are _____ and _____ .
4 Karen and Lucy are _____ and _____ .
5 Damian and Mandy are _____ and _____ .
6 Mandy and Lucy are _____ and _____ .
7 Michael and David are _____ and _____ .
8 Eve and David are _____ and _____ .
9 Lucy and David are _____ .
10 Michael / Karen and Mark / Lucy are _____ and _____ .

2 (4.4) Listen and check. Practise saying the words.

3 **pronunciation** *Son* is pronounced /sʌn/. Find seven more words with this /ʌ/ sound.

4 (4.5) **natural English** Read the box below, then listen. Are the sentences the same?

> **natural English**
> **asking about family**
>
> **Have you got** any brothers and sisters?
> Yeah, **I've got** two brothers and a sister.
> **Have you got** any children?
> No, **I haven't**.

5 Write four sentences about yourself.

    examples I've got two brothers and a sister.
               I haven't got any children.

6 Ask people about their families, using the questions in the **natural English** box.

grammar *my*, *your*, etc.

1 Look at the family tree on the left. Find two mistakes in the sentences below.

*This is me with **my** twin sister, Mandy.*

*This is our sister, Susie, with **her** husband, Richard.*

*This is **our** cousin, Michael, **his** wife, Karen, and **their** children, Lucy and Mark.*

2 Complete the table with the words in bold in **exercise 1.**

subject	possessive adjective	
I	_____ sister	Remember:
You	*your* husband	
He	_____ daughter	• use *his* when a man has
She	_____ brother	something,
It	*its* name	*Michael* and **his** *daughter*
We	_____ father	(NOT ~~her daughter~~)
They	_____ son	• use *her* when a woman has
		something,
		Karen and **her** *husband* (NOT
		~~his husband~~)

3 With a partner, write *his*, *her*, *their* in the blue boxes, and the correct names in the green boxes.

1 RICHARD: _____ girlfriend's name is _____ .

2 KAREN: _____ children's names are _____ and _____ .

3 MICHAEL: _____ daughter's name is _____ .

4 MANDY: _____ twin sister's name is _____ , and _____ husband's name is _____ .

5 CAROLE AND MANDY: _____ brother's name is _____ , and _____ niece's name is _____ .

go to **language reference** *and* **practice exercises** *p.134*

listen to this

tune in

1 Listen to Mandy. What <u>new</u> information does she give?

listen carefully

2 Read the sentences, then listen to the whole conversation. Circle the correct sentences.

1 Mandy(s got)/ hasn't got a lot of cousins.

2 Her husband is (an actor)/ a waiter.

3 She works in a school / (university.)

4 She teaches German / (computer studies.)

5 She sees her parents (Monday to Friday)/ at the weekend.

listening challenge

3 Listen and answer.

1 Has Carole got a boyfriend? *Yes*

2 What does she do? *She teaches computer studies.*

listen again with the **tapescript** *p.149*

4 **natural English.** Listen. Notice the pronunciation of *together*. Practise the sentences.

natural English
(do something) together
/təˈgeðə/

My sister and I live **together**. (= in the same house)
My brother and father work **together**. (= do the same job OR work in the same place)
Can we have lunch **together** on Saturday? (= you and me)

5 What about your family / friends? Tell a partner three things you do together.

example my family – we usually have dinner together

speaking it's your turn!

1 Write the names of three people in your family.

Olivia   Marco   Sofia

2 Work with a partner. Ask about the names they wrote.

Who's Marco?   How old …?

… married?   … boyfriend / girlfriend?

… children?   Where … live?

Where … work / study?   … like doing?

3 Find a new partner. Tell them about one member of your first partner's family.

Fabio's got a cousin called Marco. He's twenty-four, and he's married …

writing

Read this example. Then write about someone in your family. Use the words in **bold**.

MARCO: Marco's my cousin. He's twenty-four **and** he's married, **but** he hasn't got any children. He lives in Sardinia with his wife and her parents. They've got a lovely flat near the sea. He works in a hotel, **and** he speaks very good English. He likes …

can you remember …

… eight more family names?
examples mother, son, …

help with pronunciation and listening

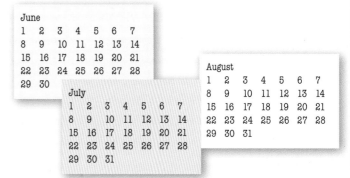
listening weak forms

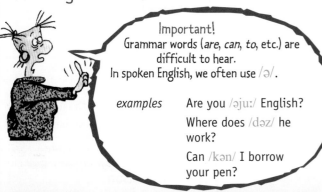

Important!
Grammar words (*are, can, to*, etc.) are difficult to hear.
In spoken English, we often use /ə/.

examples Are you /əjuː/ English?

Where does /dəz/ he work?

Can /kən/ I borrow your pen?

1 (4.11) **Listen and answer the questions.**

1 What's the time in conversation 1?

2 When's the bank open on Saturday?

3 When does the train leave?

4 When does school start?

2 Complete the sentences.

1 Excuse me, _____ _____ got _____ time, please?

2 How _____ I help you?

3 _____ you open on Saturdays?

4 _____ nine _____ four-thirty.

5 The train now leaves _____ 8.20.

6 When _____ school start?

3 Listen to 4.11 again and check. Notice the pronunciation of the missing words. Practise with a partner.

4 natural English Find these phrases in the tapescript on *p.149*. Then practise conversations 1 and 2 with a partner.

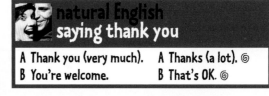

natural English
saying thank you

A Thank you (very much).   A Thanks (a lot). ◎

B You're welcome.   B That's OK. ◎

four review

grammar present simple with frequency adverbs

go to **pairwork** *p.121*

vocabulary time phrases with prepositions

1 Work with a partner. A – complete the sentences below. B – complete the sentences on *p.120*.

student A

1 My brother's birthday's on the first _____ June.
2 Do you usually go on holiday _____ July or August?
3 He's on his way to work at _____ moment.
4 See you _____ six o'clock on Sunday.
5 Do you usually have breakfast late _____ the weekend?
6 The supermarket closes at nine o'clock _____ Friday.

2 A student – find a B student. Take turns to read your sentences aloud. Are they the same?

vocabulary families

1 Make words from the jumbled letters.

~~thermo~~ = *mother*	steris	glirdneifr	sinouc
lecun	drilchen	phewen	fiew	deartugh

2 Complete the pairs with words from the box.

1 father and *mother*
2 son and _____
3 aunt and _____
4 husband and _____
5 brother and _____
6 niece and _____
7 boyfriend and _____
8 parents and _____

natural English

1 Put one missing word in each question.

example How do you get ^to school?
1 Do you work eight hours day?
2 Do you TV ten hours a week?
3 Have you got any and sisters?
4 Do you sleep seven a night?
5 Your aunts and uncles got any children?
6 You and your parents live together?

2 Check your answers with the teacher.

3 Ask and answer the questions with a partner.

---

test yourself!

Now cover the REVIEW section and test yourself on unit four.

test your vocabulary

From this unit:

1 complete these family words:
   ni _ _ _, pa _ _ _ _ s,
   gr _ _ _ _ _ _, wi _ _,
   ne _ _ _ _, co _ _ _ _,
   un _ _ _
2 write the correct preposition:
   _ *July,* _ *December 31st,*
   _ *Monday,* _ *the weekend,*
   _ *6.30*
3 match the verbs and nouns:
   (verbs) *have, read, go to, leave, watch*
   (nouns) *home, TV, lunch, the paper, bed*

score [17]

gap-fill

Fill the gaps.

1 Have you got _____ brothers and sisters?
2 **A** Thank you very much.
   B You're _____.
3 This is John and Lucy and _____ children, Julian and Tita.
4 I hardly _____ go swimming.

score [4]

error correction

Correct the errors.

1 She goes often to the cinema.
2 I can see John and her wife.
3 He always has the lunch at one o'clock.
4 I watch TV about two hours for night.

score [4]

total score [25]

Look back at the unit contents on *p.31*. Tick ✓ the language you can use.

reading
breakfast time

vocabulary breakfast food

1 Match words in the table with things in the picture.
   example 1 = coffee

a ham	eggs	sausages
b cereals	coffee	cornflakes
c rolls	bread	sugar
d butter	toast	cheese
e tea	orange juice	cake
f bacon	honey	jam

2   **pronunciation** Listen and practise.

3 Work with a partner. Which word is different in each line?

   example ham, eggs, and sausages *Eggs are different – ham and sausages are meat.*

4 **5.2** **natural English** Listen and practise with a partner.

natural English
What do you have for ...?

What do you have for	breakfast?	I usually **have** toast.
	lunch?	I sometimes **have** a sandwich.
	dinner?	I often **have** pasta.

5 Ask three people what they have for breakfast.

grammar countable and uncountable nouns

1 Look at the examples. Complete the phrases below with *a / an* or *some*.

countable singular	countable plural	uncountable (singular)
a sausage	*some* sausages / *two* sausages	–
an apple	*some* apples / *two* apples	–
–	–	*some* sugar (NOT ~~some sugars~~)

1 _____ ham	5 _____ cheese
2 _____ sandwich	6 _____ roll
3 _____ butter	7 _____ sausages
4 _____ egg	8 _____ toast

2 Look at the picture in **vocabulary exercise 1**. Find:

some coffee, and **a cup of** coffee
some juice, and **a glass of** juice
some bread, and **a piece of** bread

3 Complete the conversations with <u>one</u> word.

1 **A** Would you like a _____ of cake?
   B Oh, yes please.

2 **A** Can I have a _____ of orange juice, please?
   B Of course.

3 **A** I'm hungry.
   B Well, have _____ bread.
   A OK. Can I have a _____ of cheese, too?

4 **A** Do you want a _____ of coffee?
   B No, thanks, but I'd like _____ water.

Practise them with a partner.

go to **language reference** *and* **practice exercises** *p.135*

grammar *some / any*

1 Write these words in the table.

eggs   ham   sandwich

	positive	negative	question
SINGULAR	I want a _____ .	I don't want a _____ .	Do you want a _____ ?
PLURAL / COUNT	I want some _____ .	I don't want any _____ .	Do you want any _____ ?
UNCOUNT	I want some _____ .	I don't want any _____ .	Do you want any _____ ?

2 Circle the correct word.

1 I want some / any sugar.

2 He doesn't want some / any tea.

3 I'd like an / some apple.

4 I haven't got some / any coffee.

5 She'd like some / any sandwiches.

6 Has she got an / any eggs?

go to **language reference** *and* **practice exercises** *p.135*

3 **Think!** Look at **vocabulary exercise 1**. Tick ✓ five things you want for breakfast tomorrow, and ~~cross out~~ five things you don't want. Tell a partner.

I want some tea, a roll, some …
I don't want any …

read on

1 Where do you have breakfast – at home? at college? at work? Why? Tell a partner.

2 Read the article. Where do Andrés and Ekaterina have breakfast?

3 Circle the correct answer.

1 In Madrid / Moscow, a lot of people have breakfast at home.

2 In Madrid / Moscow, a lot of people have breakfast at 11.00.

3 In Madrid / Moscow, cornflakes aren't cheap.

4 In Madrid / Moscow, you can have wine for breakfast.

5 Andrés / Ekaterina drinks tea and eats jam with it.

6 Ekaterina has / doesn't have breakfast with her family.

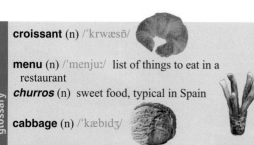

glossary

croissant (n) /ˈkrwæsɒ̃/

menu (n) /ˈmenjuː/ list of things to eat in a restaurant

churros (n) sweet food, typical in Spain

cabbage (n) /ˈkæbɪdʒ/

(be) in a hurry (n) /ˈhʌri/ do something quickly

porridge (n) /ˈpɒrɪdʒ/ a hot food made from cereal and milk or water

round the world at 8.00 a.m.

MADRID

'8.00's very early for breakfast!' says Antonio Romero, manager of 'La Taurina', a bar in the centre of Madrid, near the Puerta del Sol. 'The most popular time for breakfast is 11.00, when people come out of their offices for coffee, toast, and **croissants**.'

But at 8.00, the bar is quiet, with only the TV on.

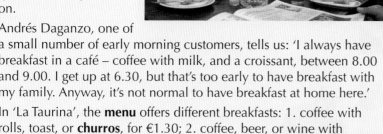

Andrés Daganzo, one of a small number of early morning customers, tells us: 'I always have breakfast in a café – coffee with milk, and a croissant, between 8.00 and 9.00. I get up at 6.30, but that's too early to have breakfast with my family. Anyway, it's not normal to have breakfast at home here.'

In 'La Taurina', the **menu** offers different breakfasts: 1. coffee with rolls, toast, or **churros**, for €1.30; 2. coffee, beer, or wine with sandwiches for €1.50. A glass of fresh orange juice is yours for €0.60.

MOSCOW

In Russia, where people usually have breakfast at home, they eat it quickly. Because of the cold weather, they eat food like sausages, cheese, eggs, and bread. Ekaterina Arutseva, a Moscow resident, tells us: 'First I give the rabbit some **cabbage** for breakfast. I turn on the radio, and my husband has a quiet cigarette. Then I make breakfast for

my husband and son, but I hardly ever have breakfast with them, because I'm always **in a hurry**. We have **porridge**, called 'kasha', which is easy, and sometimes we have food from dinner the night before. I like to drink tea and we eat jam or honey with the tea. My son would like to have the cornflakes he sees on TV, but they're very expensive here.'

speaking it's your turn!

1 **Think!** Think about your answers.

What time do you usually have breakfast?

Where, and who with?

What do you have for breakfast?

Are you usually in a hurry?

Do you do other things at breakfast time? e.g. listen to the radio

Is your breakfast different at the weekend? If so, how?

2 **Ask three students. Are they similar to you?**

> What time do you usually have breakfast?

writing

1 Read about Celine. Does she answer all the questions in **it's your turn, exercise 1**?

Celine, France

I usually have breakfast at home at about 8.00 with my family. I have cereals first, then bread and butter and jam, and lots of coffee. I only have ten minutes for breakfast. During breakfast, I talk to the family and sometimes I watch the news on TV. At the weekend, I have breakfast late, at about 10.00. I sometimes go to a café and meet friends there.

2 Write about yourself. Use the questions in **it's your turn!** and Celine's text to help you.

can you remember ...

... the things in the picture on *p.39*? Say the words with *a / an* or *some*.

wordbooster

food

1 Complete the words.

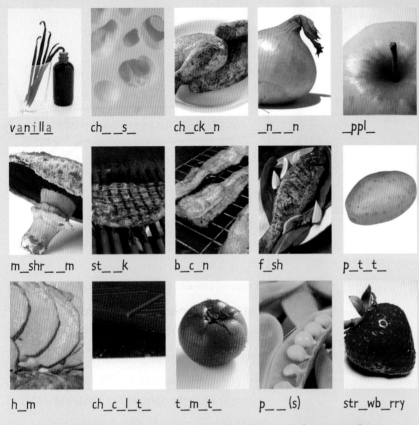

vanilla   ch__s_   ch_ck_n   _n__n   _ppl_

m_shr__m   st__k   b_c_n   f_sh   p_t_t_

h_m   ch_c_l_t_   t_m_t_   p___(s)   str_wb_rry

2 With a partner, complete the phrases with words from exercise 1.

cheese
_____ sandwich   _____ soup   _____ ice cream

_____ and chips   _____ tart
_____ (also french fries)

3 **pronunciation** From exercises 1 and 2, find:
five words with the /ɪ/ sound, e.g. *sit*
three words with the /iː/ sound, e.g. *see*
three words with the /eɪ/ sound, e.g. *say*
three words with the /æ/ sound, e.g. *bag*

4  **5.3** Listen and check your answers.
Practise the words.

5 **5.4** **natural English** Listen and fill the
gaps. Then practise with a partner.

> **natural English**
> *What kind of ...?*
>
> **What kind of** _____ have you got?
> It's onion or mushroom.
> **What kind of** _____ do you like?
> Well, chocolate's my favourite.

6 Ask your partner what kind of soup,
sandwiches, and ice cream they like.

adjectives (2)

1 Complete with opposites from the box.

uncomfortable	slow	expensive
unfriendly	dirty /'dɜːti/	awful /'ɔːfl/

		☺	☹
		THE LAKE CAFÉ	THE RIVER RESTAURANT
FOOD		excellent!	_____
PLACE		clean	_____
		comfortable /'kʌmftəbl/	_____
SERVICE		fast	_____
PRICES		cheap	_____
ATMOSPHERE		friendly /'frendli/	_____

2 Look at the table for one minute. Then
close your book. Tell a partner what you can
remember.

3 **5.5** Listen to Candida and Jonathan.
What do they say about their
favourite restaurants?

listening
how to... order food

can you remember ...
... three kinds of sandwich, three kinds of ice cream, and three kinds of meat? Tell a partner.

grammar *can / can't* + verb

1 Read the text. Then match pictures a to c with paragraphs 1 to 3.

2 Underline the correct answer.

1 In the early morning, you can get coffee in:
   a a bar   b a café   c a restaurant
2 You can't get alcoholic drinks in:
   a a bar   b a café   c a restaurant
3 You can't watch TV in:
   a a bar   b a café   c a restaurant
4 You can have an alcoholic drink without eating in:
   a a bar   b a café   c a restaurant

3 Circle the correct word.

You can / can't = It's possible.   You can / can't = It's not possible.

4 Cover the text. Complete these sentences about Britain using *can / can't* + verb.

1 You *can watch* TV in a bar.
2 You _____ _____ a paper in a café.
3 You _____ _____ TV in a restaurant.
4 You _____ _____ coffee in a restaurant without eating.
5 You _____ _____ friends in a bar.
6 You _____ _____ dinner in a restaurant.
7 You _____ _____ wine in a café.

5 (5.6) **pronunciation** Listen. Do you hear *can* /kən/ or *can't* /kɑːnt/? Say the sentences in **exercise 4**.

6 With a partner, say sentences using *can / can't* about bars, cafés, and restaurants in your country.

go to **language reference** *and* **practice exercises** *p.136*

7 **Think!** Think about your favourite café, bar, or restaurant.

Where is it?   When do you go there?
Who do you go with?   What can you do there?
What can you get to eat or drink?   Why do you like it?

Talk in small groups. Which is the best place?

In Britain:

a

1 A CAFÉ is a place where you *can* **get** coffee, sandwiches, and other **snacks** from early morning to early evening. You *can* meet friends there and read the paper. You *can't* usually get alcoholic drinks in a café.

2 A RESTAURANT is a place where you *can* get lunch or dinner and have beer or wine. You *can't* drink in a restaurant without eating, and you *can't* usually watch TV in a restaurant. You pay **the bill** at the end.

3 A PUB OR BAR, which is usually open from 11.00 a.m., is a place where you *can* meet friends and have a drink. You *can* have beer, wine, and usually tea or coffee at lunchtime. In some bars you *can* watch TV and you *can* usually *get* something to eat. You pay when you order.

b

c

glossary
get (sth to eat / drink) (v) buy
snack (n) a small meal e.g. a burger
the bill (n) what you pay for food and drink in a restaurant

listen to this
tune in

1 (5.7) **natural English** Listen and complete the dialogue.

natural English
ordering food

Waiter	What would you like?
Customer	**I'll have** _____ , _____ . (NOT I have)
Waiter	OK. **Anything else?**
Customer	No, _____ all, thanks.

2 **pronunciation** Listen again and notice the pronunciation of *I'll* /aɪl/. Practise the dialogue with a partner.

listen carefully

3 Look at the pictures. What you can see? Tell a partner.

4 (5.8) Listen. What does the woman order? Choose the correct picture. Does she have anything else?

5 Listen again. Complete the waiter's questions. Practise them.
1 _____ potatoes or French fries with that?
2 _____ to drink?

listening challenge

6 (5.9) **natural English.** Listen and complete the questions. Practise the dialogues with a partner.

natural English
asking for more

Woman	Can I have _____ glass of wine, please?
Waiter	Sure.
Woman	Can I have _____ _____ water, please?
Waiter	Yes, of course.

7 Why does she say *another* glass of wine, but *some more* water?

8 Write *another* or *some more*.
1 _____ bread
2 _____ glass of orange juice
3 _____ jam
4 _____ cup of coffee
5 _____ soup
6 _____ bottle of water

Listen again with the **tapescript** *p.150.*

speaking it's your turn!

1 Work with a partner. You are waiters. Prepare the questions.

Say hello
What ... like?
... potatoes or chips?
... salad?
What ... drink?
Anything else?

2 Practise the conversation with your partner.

A – you are the waiter.

B – you are the customer. You decide what you want.

Hello. What would you ...?

can you remember ...

... three questions a waiter can ask, and three questions a customer can ask?

extended speaking

what's on the menu?

you're going to:

collect ideas	prepare a menu	role play
talk about a café you know	prepare and write a menu	act out a situation in the café

 ## collect ideas

1 **Think!** Think about a café / snack bar in or near your school.

What can you eat and drink there?

Is it cheap, expensive, or OK?

What do you think of the café?

Tell a partner.

prepare a menu

2 You have a café. Look at the menu. With your partner, think of:

- a name for your café
- your food and drinks
- prices
- something special about your café, e.g. you can use the Internet; you can have a free drink with your meal

3 Together, complete your menus. (You need one copy each.)

role play

4 Work with a new partner.

A You are a <u>waiter / waitress</u>. Give the customers your menu. Take the order, then serve the food and drink.

B You are a <u>customer</u>. Order from the menu. Eat your food, then ask for something else.

5 Change roles and repeat the activity.

6 Go back to your first partner. Tell them about the café you visited. What did you think of:

– the food and drink?   – the service?

– the special feature?   – the prices?

.... CAFÉ MENU

hot food	price
....	....
....	....
....	....
cold food	**price**
....	....
....	....
....	....
....	....
hot drinks	**price**
....	....
....	....
....	....
....	....
cold drinks	**price**
....	....
....	....
....	....
....	....

SPECIAL!

....

five review

vocabulary food

1 Work in A / B pairs.

A Complete your part of the crossword below.

B Go to *p.121*.

CLUES ACROSS →

2 _____ and eggs

5 you put it on bread; it's made from fruit

7 a _____ of cake

8 fish and _____

9 an alcoholic drink

13 a vegetable

14 lunch and dinner are _____

15 ice _____

16 'A _____ of coffee, please.'

2 Read your clues to your partner. They write the answers in their crossword.

grammar *can / can't* (possibility)

1 You have <u>three</u> minutes. With a partner, write down:

two things you can do in: – a restaurant   – a bookshop   – a hotel

two things you can't do: – in your class   – on a plane

2 Read your answers to another pair. Are their answers the same?

 natural English

1 Put <u>one</u> missing word in each line.

Waiter	Good morning. What ^would you like?
Customer	I'll have black coffee, please, and piece of cake.
Waiter	Sure. What kind cake?
Customer	Er ... chocolate. And can I a glass of water?
Waiter	Of course. Anything?
Customer	No, that all, thank you.

2 Check your answers using the **natural English** boxes in unit five. Then practise the dialogue.

grammar countable and uncountable nouns

go to **pairwork** *p.122*

test yourself!

Now cover the REVIEW section and test yourself on unit five.

test your vocabulary

From this unit:

1 write five phrases, using a different word each time: *vanilla* _____ ; *chicken* _____ ; *strawberry* _____ ; _____ *and chips; a* _____ *sandwich*

2 write the opposite of: *clean, fast, comfortable, awful, friendly*

3 complete these uncountable food and drink words: bu _ _ _ _ , ch _ _ _ _ , co _ _ _ _ , so _ _ , br _ _ _ , su _ _ _ , to _ _ _

score [17]

gap-fill

Fill the gaps.

1 We haven't got _____ bread.

2 Do you want a _____ of cake?

3 Can I have _____ more coffee, please?

4 What _____ of wine do you want?

score [4]

error correction

Correct the errors.

1 I'd like any cheese.

2 What do you have for the breakfast?

3 Waiter: What would you like?
Customer: I have steak and chips, please.

4 Can I have more one glass of water, please?

score [4]

total score [25]

Look back at the unit contents on *p.39*. Tick ✓ the language you can use.

reading
a day out

vocabulary tourist places

1 **6.1** Complete the words. Then listen and practise.

1

chu _ _ _

2

cas _ _ _

3

sta _ _ _

4

squ _ _ _

5

cathed _ _ _

6

bri _ _ _

7

mus _ _ _

8

mar _ _ _

9

pal _ _ _

10

fount _ _ _

2 With a partner, write an example of <u>eight</u> of the places above (in your town or the world).

examples Charles Bridge in Prague
The Flower Market in Amsterdam
The British Museum in London

Read your answers to another pair. How many are the same?

grammar past simple *was* / *were*

1 **6.2** Listen to these tourists talking about a bus tour of Brighton. Complete the speech bubbles.

An hour was about right, and it was a very interesting _____.

The bus wasn't very _____, but the tour guide was _____.

The people on the bus were all _____ and the driver was really funny.

The weather wasn't very _____ but we were _____.

2 Underline the verbs in the past tense.

3 Complete these sentences.

1 *Was* and *were* are past forms of the verb _____ .

2 For *I, he, she, it*, use _____ . For *we, you, they*, use _____ .
  examples   He _____ late yesterday.
               We _____ at school last Monday.

3 _____ / *were* are positive, and _____ / *weren't* are negative.
  examples   I _____ a tour guide for two years. We _____ happy with the food – it was terrible.

4 **6.3** **pronunciation** Listen. Circle the word you hear.

1 I was / wasn't here yesterday.
2 She's / was very tired this morning.
3 The market was / wasn't very interesting.
4 They were / weren't here last summer.
5 We were / weren't in the same class last year.
6 **A** Is / Was Jack at home?   **B** Yes, I think he is / was.

5 With a partner, complete these questions with names of people in your class. The answer can be 'yes' or 'no'.

example   Was *Kiko* late for class today?

1 Was _____ late for class today?
2 Was _____ at home last night?
3 Was _____ in the same place / seat in the last lesson?
4 Were _____ and _____ in class in the last lesson?
5 Was _____ in a café or a restaurant before the lesson?
6 Were _____ and _____ in class in the last lesson?

6 Find a new partner. Ask and try to answer the questions.

go to **language reference** *and* **practice exercises** *p.136*

read on

1 With a partner, tick ✓ <u>three</u> things you think are important.

A good tour guide:
- ☐ is interesting
- ☐ knows a lot
- ☐ is funny
- ☐ speaks different languages
- ☐ likes people
- ☐ is friendly
- ☐ is young
- ☐ looks nice

Compare with another pair.

I'm a guide

Matthew Roberts, 25, works as a guide on tour buses in London. He's an actor, but it's very difficult for young actors to find work, so he does this for extra money.

With the microphone in his hand, Matthew gives more of a show than a tour.

'They say small people always do well,' he begins, as the bus moves slowly round Trafalgar Square. 'Lord Nelson and Napoleon, for example, were both small: Nelson was 142cms, and Napoleon, Emperor of France, was 137cms. I'm 185cms – and I work on a bus!'

People don't always understand his **jokes**, but everyone likes his tours, and Matthew certainly knows lots of interesting facts. 'That's a statue of Queen Anne,' he says. 'She had 17 children. And that's the **famous** Ritz Hotel – Hollywood stars Charlie Chaplin and Cary Grant both worked there. And there's the Pall Mall Hotel – Vietnamese President Ho Chi Minh was a **chef** there. Oh, and that's Buckingham Palace, where my **ex-girlfriend** works. She was horrible to me. Let's all **shout**, 'Clare! You were stupid to finish with Matthew!' Immediately the tourists all stand up and shout across the street, 'Clare! You were stupid to finish with Matthew!'

'Some people are only here for 24 hours,' says Matthew, 'but I want them to leave London happy.'

2 Read the article about Matthew Roberts. Is he a good tour guide?

3 Complete these facts with the correct name.

1 _____ is an actor.
2 _____ was a chef at the Pall Mall Hotel.
3 _____ and _____ were very short.
4 _____ and _____ worked at the Ritz Hotel.
5 _____ had lots of children.
6 _____ was Matthew's girlfriend.

4 Would you like to be a tour guide or an actor? Why / Why not? Talk in small groups.

5 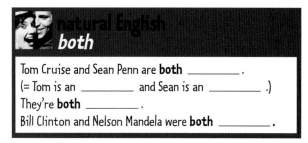 **natural English** Complete the sentences, then listen and check.

> **natural English**
> ***both***
>
> Tom Cruise and Sean Penn are **both** _____.
> (= Tom is an _____ and Sean is an _____.)
> They're **both** _____.
> Bill Clinton and Nelson Mandela were **both** _____.

6 Find two more examples of *both* in the article.

7 With a partner, make sentences about the people / things in the wordpool using *both*.

example   Julius Caesar and Leonardo da Vinci were **both** Italian.

Julius Caesar   Halle Berry   Chianti
Paul McCartney   The Louvre   Al Pacino
Leonardo da Vinci   Pelé   Stalin   Nelson
Donald Duck   Maradona   sake
spaghetti   Mickey Mouse
The Prado   Lenin   lasagne
John Lennon   Napoleon

speaking it's your turn!

1 **Think!** Think about a day out in the past, e.g. a day at the beach, a sightseeing tour.

Where were you?
When was it?
Who were you with?
Why were you there?
Was the weather good / OK / terrible?
Was it great / interesting / OK / boring? Why?

2 Tell a partner about your day.

> So tell me about your day ... where were you?

can you remember ...

... ten tourist places? Tell a partner.

glossary

joke (n) short, funny story
famous (adj) /ˈfeɪməs/ thing / person that a lot of people know about, e.g. The Taj Mahal, Nelson Mandela
chef (n) /ʃef/ person who cooks food in a restaurant / hotel
ex-girlfriend (n) girlfriend in the past, but not now
shout (v) /ʃaʊt/ speak in a loud voice

wordbooster

past time phrases

1 Complete the phrases. Use words from the box.

evening	week	1998	ten days
year	afternoon	morning	night
a few days	a week	month	2005

yesterday
_____
_____
_____

last
_____
_____
_____
_____

_____
_____ ago
_____

in
_____
_____

2 **Think!** Where were you:
- last night?
- yesterday afternoon?
- yesterday morning?
- four weeks ago?
- last year?
- in 1998?

Tell a partner.

verb + noun collocation

1 Match the verbs and nouns.

go	at home
wash	with friends
go	for a walk
stay	nothing
do	shopping
go out	cards
play	to a party
meet	the flat
clean	a friend for a drink
go	homework
do	the car

2 Match each phrase with a picture.

3 **Think!** Which of the activities do you often / hardly ever / never do?

examples I often go shopping with my sister.

I hardly ever play cards.

Talk about your answers in small groups.

listening
how to...talk about last weekend

lead-in

1 Work in groups. What's your favourite day of the week? Why?

2 **natural English** Match a to d with 1 to 4.

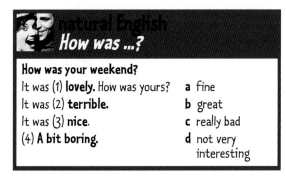

natural English
How was ...?

How was your weekend?

It was (1) **lovely.** How was yours?	**a** fine
It was (2) **terrible.**	**b** great
It was (3) **nice.**	**c** really bad
(4) **A bit boring.**	**d** not very interesting

3 (6.5) **pronunciation** Listen and copy the intonation. Then practise the conversations with three people.

grammar past simple regular and irregular verbs

1 People write about their lives on 'weblogs' on the Internet. Read the ones opposite. Write these sentences in the correct place.

My weekend was OK, but a bit boring.

The children loved it.

That was a bit boring too.

I had a lovely weekend.

2 Which weekend do you prefer – Max's or Margaret's? Tell a partner.

3 Find seven regular verbs in the weblogs. Write them in the box.

regular past tense	+ed	+d
	clean**ed**	lik**ed**

4 (6.6) **pronunciation** Listen and practise. Notice the pronunciation of *wanted* /ˈwɒntɪd/ **and** *deci**ded*** /dɪˈsaɪdɪd/.

www.weblog.com   Q▾ Google

Margaret

1 _____ . On Friday my daughter wanted to go shopping, and we bought lots of things for our holiday. On Saturday morning, I cleaned the house and played with my son, Chip. We went to my sister June's for her birthday lunch and saw her new house. I really liked it – it was fantastic. When we got home we watched a DVD together (Shrek, as usual). 2 _____ .

www.weblog.com   Q▾ Google

Max

3 _____ . Marina and I stayed at home on Friday night, played cards, and watched a DVD (we thought it was terrible). On Saturday, I did NOTHING. All day. Sunday was a nice day. I decided to go for a walk – and I WASHED the car! YES! First time in a year. In the evening, I met my brother in town for a drink. 4 _____ .

5 Complete the table with irregular verbs from the weblogs.

irregular verbs infinitive	past simple	test your partner – Do?
have	_____	
buy	_____ /bɔːt/	
go	_____	– Did.
see	_____ /sɔː/	
get	_____	– Yes.
think	_____ /θɔːt/	
do	_____	
meet	_____	

6 Complete the sentences in the past simple.

1 Margaret _____ a lovely weekend.

2 Her daughter _____ to go shopping.

3 They _____ a lot of things.

4 She _____ to her sister's and _____ her new house.

5 Max _____ at home on Friday and _____ a DVD.

6 He _____ the DVD was terrible.

7 On Sunday he _____ to go for a walk and he _____ the car.

8 In the evening, he _____ his brother for a drink.

7 Work with a partner:

A – you are Margaret.

B – you are Max.

Close your book. Talk about your weekend:

Max – How was your weekend?

Margaret – I had a lovely weekend. I ...

go to **language reference** *and* **practice exercises** *p.137*

listen to this

Tyler

Juliet

Federay

tune in

1 (6.7) Listen to the beginning of two conversations. Did Juliet and Tyler both have a good weekend?

listen carefully

Juliet		Tyler	
Saturday evening	_____	Saturday evening	_____
Sunday morning 1	_____	Sunday morning 1	_____
2	_____	2	_____

2 Listen to Juliet and Tyler. Complete their diaries.

3 With a partner, make sentences about Juliet and Tyler's weekends.

listening challenge

4 (6.8) Listen to Federay. What did she do last weekend, and what did she think of it? Tell a partner.

listen again with the **tapescript** *p.150*

5 **natural English** Find the **natural English** phrases in bold in tapescript 6.7 and 6.8 on *p.150*. How do you say these in your language?

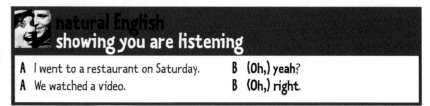

natural English
showing you are listening

| A | I went to a restaurant on Saturday. | B | (Oh,) yeah? |
| A | We watched a video. | B | (Oh,) right. |

speaking it's your turn!

1 **Think!** How was your weekend? What did you do? Make notes. Use a dictionary or ask your teacher if necessary.

On Friday evening ...

On Saturday (morning / afternoon / evening) ...

On Sunday (morning / afternoon / evening)...

2 Ask three people about their weekend.

How was your weekend?

It was great. On Friday I went to ...

writing

Write a weblog about your weekend. Use Margaret's and Max's to help you.

can you remember ...

... the past tense of these verbs?

be _____ have _____ do _____ decide _____

go _____ buy _____ meet _____ get _____

help with pronunciation and listening

pronunciation sounds /ɔː/, /ɜː/, and /ɒ/

1 Complete the phrases in the table with these words. The <u>underlined</u> sounds must be the same.

w<u>or</u>k   w<u>a</u>sh   w<u>a</u>lk

/ɔː/	/ɜː/	/ɒ/
a m<u>or</u>ning _____	d<u>ir</u>ty _____	a h<u>o</u>t _____

2 Which <u>underlined</u> sound is different? Work with a partner.

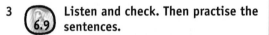

example   I <u>o</u>ften have a m<u>or</u>ning w<u>a</u>lk.
(different / same / same)

1 Th<u>ur</u>sday the f<u>ir</u>st of <u>Au</u>gust.
2 I s<u>aw</u> him <u>ear</u>ly this m<u>or</u>ning.
3 Wh<u>a</u>t do you w<u>a</u>nt to l<u>ear</u>n?
4 My d<u>au</u>ghter w<u>a</u>lked to the sh<u>o</u>ps.
5 I b<u>ou</u>ght some m<u>ore</u> c<u>o</u>ffee.
6 We start w<u>or</u>k at f<u>our</u>-th<u>ir</u>ty.

3 (6.9) Listen and check. Then practise the sentences.

4 Write the words in blue in the correct column in the table in exercise 1.

listening prediction (1)

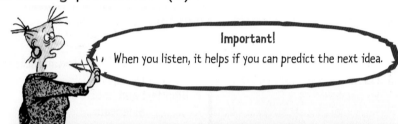

> **Important!**
> When you listen, it helps if you can predict the next idea.

1 Deri is late for a business meeting with Conrad in Oxford. With a partner, think of four or five possible reasons why.

example   Maybe he had a problem with his car.

2 (6.10) Listen. Why was he late? Was it one of your reasons?

3 When Deri arrived at Oxford station, he had another problem. With your partner, think of three possible problems.

(6.11) Listen. Were you right?

4 Di is meeting Carl, and she's late. She went shopping and had two problems. With your partner, think of three possible problems.

5 (6.12) Listen. Were you right?

6 natural English Complete the conversation. Then check in tapescripts 6.10, 6.11 and 6.12 on p.150.

natural English
saying sorry

A Hello.
B Oh hi. Look, (I'm) (really) sorry _____ late. (NOT ~~to be late~~)
A That's OK. _____ worry.

Practise with your partner.

listen again with the tapescript p.150

six review

grammar past simple and past time phrases

1 Write sentence endings that are true for you.

1 Last night I …

2 Yesterday morning I …

3 A few days ago I …

4 Last week I …

5 Last year I …

6 In 2004 I …

2 Read your sentence endings to a partner. They guess the correct time phrase.

example   **A** I left school.

　　　　　B In 2004?

　　　　　A No, last year.

vocabulary past time phrases, verb + noun collocation

Cross out the <u>wrong</u> answer.

example   We went a walk / for a walk.

1 I went out with my brother yesterday evening / night.

2 She saw them a few days ago / ago a few days.

3 We met her last week / the last week.

4 They lived here on / in 2002.

5 I stayed in / at home last night.

6 I must do / make my homework.

7 We can go shopping / to shopping.

8 They went home / at home after the lesson.

natural English

1 Fill the gaps with one word. (Contractions, e.g. *he's*, are one word.)

1 **A** I'm sorry _____ late.

　B That's OK. Don't _____ .

2 **A** _____ was your weekend?

　B Very _____ . How _____ yours?

　A Oh, it was a _____ boring.

3 **A** Is Ana married?

　B Yes.

　A And Laura?

　B Yes. They're _____ married.

2 Check your answers using the **natural English** boxes in unit six.

grammar past simple verbs

go to **pairwork** *p.120*

---

test yourself!

Now cover the REVIEW section and test yourself on unit six.

test your vocabulary

From this unit, write down:

1 seven places in a town: *latesc, alapec, taderchla, rakmet, huccrh, drigeb, umsuem*

2 four past time phrases using these words: *last, ago, night, 2005, a week, yesterday, in, evening*

3 six nouns to complete these phrases: *go out with _____ , play _____ , wash the _____ , go _____ , stay at _____ , go for a _____*

score   17

gap-fill

Fill the gaps.

1 **A** Where _____ you last night?
  B In town.

2 Brad Pitt and Robert de Niro are _____ American.

3 She _____ out with friends last night.

4 I saw Jack three months _____ .

score   4

error correction

Correct the errors.

1 I do a lot of homework last night.

2 We decide to stay at home yesterday.

3 Was you late for school this morning?

4 She buy the car in 2004.

score 4

total score 25

Look back at the unit contents on *p.47*. Tick ✓ the language you can use.

tick ✓ when you know this

natural English
- [ ] link words: *then / after that*
- [ ] *quite* and *very*
- [ ] *What's he / she like?*
- [ ] *When did you last ...?*

grammar
- [ ] past simple negatives
- [ ] past simple questions
- [ ] object pronouns

vocabulary
- [ ] life story
- [ ] appearance
- [ ] character

reading
biographies

vocabulary life story

1 Complete the sentences about Kay with phrases from the box.

school at 18	a baby	~~in 1965~~	in a small village
in a school in Scotland	to university	a teacher	to an engineer

my life story	Kay Jacobs
1 I was born	*in 1965*.
2 I grew up	_____.
3 I left	_____.
4 I went	_____.
5 I became	_____.
6 I worked	_____.
7 I got married	_____.
8 I had	_____.

2 **7.1** Listen and check. Practise the sentences.

3 What are the infinitive forms of the verbs in **exercise 1**?

example **was** born – be born

grammar past simple negatives

1 🔊 7.2 Listen to Mike. Complete the conversation.

Jill Are the sentences true for you?

Mike Well, most of them, no. I _____ born in 1965, and I didn't grow up in a small village. I grew up in Liverpool.

Jill What about your education?

Mike Different again. I _____ leave school at 18, and I _____ _____ to university. In fact, I _____ school at 16 and _____ a job.

2 Compare with a partner, then check with the tapescript on *p.150*.

3 Complete the table.

PAST SIMPLE positive	negative
I worked there.	I didn't work there.
You wanted it.	You _____ _____ it.
He got the job.	He _____ _____ the job.
She bought the book.	She _____ _____ the book.
We went there yesterday.	We _____ _____ there yesterday.
They did it.	They _____ _____ it.

4 Practise the negative form in A / B pairs. A – go to *p.123*. B – go to *p.120*.

5 Look at the sentences in **vocabulary exercise 1** on *p.55*. Are they true for you? Tell a partner.

example

I wasn't born in 1965 – I was born in 1984.

I grew up in a small village. That's true.

go to **language reference** *and* **practice exercises** *p.137*

read on

1 What do you know about 'Harry Potter' and the writer, J K Rowling? Tell a partner.

2 Read the text. How many jobs did she have before she was famous?

Before she was famous ...

J K Rowling was born near Bristol in 1965. She always wanted to be a writer, and her first book was called *Rabbit*, which she wrote when she was six years old. She grew up in a town in the south-west of England, and when she left school, she went to Exeter University. After that, she **moved** to London and worked for Amnesty International.

She first had the idea for a Harry Potter book in 1990 when she was on a long train journey. But in the same year, she went to Oporto in Portugal and worked as an English teacher. When she was there, she met a Portuguese journalist – they got married and had a baby. **Unfortunately**, the marriage wasn't a long one and she left, with her baby daughter, in 1993. She came back to Britain and lived in a small flat in Edinburgh. She was **unemployed** and didn't have much money, but she continued writing. She also did a teaching course and then became a French teacher in a school in Edinburgh. In 1997, *Harry Potter and the Philosopher's Stone* was published.

Rowling's first three books **sold** over 35 million copies in three years, and in 2001 Chris Columbus made the first Harry Potter film. J K Rowling still lives in Edinburgh.

glossary

move (v) /muːv/ leave one home to live in another
unfortunately (adv) /ʌnˈfɔːtʃənətli/ a word that introduces bad or sad news
unemployed (adj) /ʌnɪmˈplɔɪd/ with no job
sold (past tense of *sell*) /səʊld/ opposite of *bought*

3 Are the sentences in **vocabulary exercise 1** true for J K Rowling? Write *yes, no,* or *not sure* in the table.

4 You have two minutes. With your partner, find ten irregular verbs in the text. Which pair can finish first?

5 **natural English** Read the box and find more examples in the text.

natural English
link words: *then / after that*

We had a drink. **Then** we went to the cinema.
OR We had a drink, **and then** we went to the cinema.
I went shopping. **After that**, I met my sister.
OR I went shopping, **and after that**, I met my sister.

6 Link pairs of sentences using the **natural English** phrases.

example I sold my computer, and *then / after that*, I bought a laptop.

I finished my homework.

~~I sold my computer.~~

I worked in Poland for a year.

We went out for a drink.

We got married six months ago.

~~I bought a laptop.~~ We bought a flat.

I went for a walk.

We played computer games.

I went to Korea.

grammar past simple questions

1 Complete the table.

past simple questions	past simple *be* questions
_____ she **go** to university?	_____ she a teacher?
Yes, she _____ .	Yes, she _____ .
Where _____ she _____ married?	_____ they happy?
She _____ married in Portugal.	No, they _____ .

2 Complete the questions with *is, does, was,* or *did.*

1 What _____ J K Rowling's first name?
2 _____ she write a book called *Rabbit*?
3 What _____ she study at university?
4 How long _____ she work in London?
5 _____ her baby born in Portugal?
6 Why _____ she leave Portugal?
7 Why _____ she move to Edinburgh?
8 Why _____ she use the name 'Potter' in her books?
9 How many books _____ she sell in the first three years?
10 _____ she get married a second time?
11 _____ she have any more children?
12 Where _____ she live now?

3 Which questions can you answer?

4 Work with a partner.   A Go to *p.123*.   B Go to *p.129*.

5 Ask your partner the questions in **exercise 2** that you can't answer.

go to **language reference** *and* **practice exercises** *p.137*

speaking it's your turn!

1 **Think!** Think of questions for a partner, using these prompts.

Did you ... ?

go on holiday last year? (If 'yes', where?)
work hard last month? (If 'yes', why?)
go to a restaurant or bar last week? (If 'yes', where? What / have?)
go shopping last weekend? (If 'yes', what / buy?)
watch TV last night? (If 'yes', what?)
go out last night? (If 'yes', where / go?)
your question _____

2 Ask your partner.

Did you go out last night?

Oh, really? Where did you go?

can you remember ...

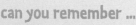

... how to say these in the negative and question forms?
They wanted to see me. (Why?)   She got married last year. (When?)   He had dinner at Nando's. (Where?)

wordbooster

appearance

1 Read the texts. Write the words in bold in the table below.

1 She's tall, **thin**, and quite attractive. She's got long **dark** hair.

2 He's **short** and a bit fat, but quite **good-looking**. He's got **short brown** hair with a **beard** and a **moustache**.

3 She's quite tall and very **beautiful**. She's got **medium-length** blonde hair.

he's ... / she's ...	
tall / _____	_____ / attractive / good-looking (women)
_____ / a bit fat	attractive / _____ (men)

he's / she's got ...	he's got ...
long dark hair	a _____
_____ _____ hair	a _____
_____ _____ hair	

2 **(7.3)** pronunciation Listen and practise the sentences.

3 natural English. Match the sentences and pictures.

natural English
quite /kwaɪt/ **and** ***very***

1 He's **quite** tall.
2 He's got **quite** long hair.
3 He's **very** tall.
4 He's got **very** long hair.

a   b   c   d

4 Write four sentences about students in your class using *quite* or *very*. Don't write the names.

example   He's quite short and very good-looking.

5 Read your sentences to a partner. Can he / she say who it is?

character

1 Match opposites from the circles.

funny /ˈfʌni/
interesting   clever
strict   hard-working
nice /naɪs/

horrible /ˈhɒrɪbl/
serious /ˈsɪəriəs/   relaxed
stupid   lazy /ˈleɪzi/
boring

test your partner
– What's the opposite of 'strict'?

– Relaxed.

– Yes.

2 Think! What do you think?

1 Are footballers usually ...
   interesting?   stupid?   lazy?
2 Are teachers usually ...
   strict?   hard-working?   funny?
3 Are doctors usually ...
   serious?   horrible?   clever?
4 Are police officers usually ...
   funny?   relaxed?   nice?
5 Are accountants usually ...
   stupid?   serious?   clever?

3 In small groups, talk about your answers.

listening

how to ... talk about people you know

lead-in

Think! What are your answers?

Have you (or your family) got a lot of photos at home or on your computer?

What kind of photos are they? e.g. friends, family, holidays, etc.

Have you got photos of you as a baby?

Do you like looking at old photos? Why / Why not?

Tell a partner.

grammar object pronouns

1 **(7.4)** Look at the photos. Listen and complete the sentences.

I work with _____ .

I work with _____ .

I met _____ last month.

That's _____ .

No! That's not _____ !

2 Complete the table with the pronouns from **exercise 1**.

subject pronoun	object pronoun	number
I	_____	
you	_____	
he	_____	
she	_____	
it	it	1
we	us	
they	_____	

3 **(7.5)** **pronunciation** Listen. Number the pronouns in the table in the order you hear them. Notice the pronunciation of *him* (/hɪm/), *her* (/hɜː/), and *them* (/ðəm/).

4 Change the words in green to pronouns.

                              her
example I didn't see ~~my sister~~ yesterday.

1 Have you got the laptop?
2 Do you know Mary's children?
3 Where did you meet Michael?
4 I put the books in the car.
5 He gave the money to Peter and me.
6 She asked Alicia a question.
7 I sold the computer last week.
8 I don't know John or David.

5 Read your sentences to a partner. Remember the pronunciation of *him*, *her*, and *them*.

go to **language reference** *and* **practice exercises** *p.138*

6 **(7.6)** **natural English** Listen. Tick ✓ the question and answer you hear. Then practise the dialogues in the box.

natural English
What's he / she like?

Use this question to ask about people's character. (*What's = What is*)

What's he like?	He's hard-working.
	He's quite funny.
	NOT ~~He's like ...~~
What's she like?	She's serious.
	She's very nice.

7 Ask your partner about his / her:

brother   sister   mother   father

What's your brother like?

listen to this

tune in

1 Look at the photos. What do they teach? Tell a partner.

2 Two people are talking about teachers they had at school. Which **two** things will they say first?

– the teacher's name

– the name of the school

– the teacher's age

– the subject he / she taught e.g. French, sport

3 Listen to the beginning of the conversations. Were you right?

listen carefully

4 Listen to the conversations and circle the correct answer.

Lynne's teacher

1 She taught English / geography.

2 She was / wasn't attractive.

3 She was clever / strict.

4 She was her teacher for two / three years.

5 Lynne liked / didn't like her.

Glen's teacher

1 She taught maths / drama.

2 She was old / young.

3 She was serious / funny.

4 She was Glen's teacher for four or five / ten years.

5 Glen liked / didn't like her.

listening challenge

5 Listen to Juliet. Tell a partner what you can remember about her teacher.

*listen again with the **tapescript** p.151*

6 **natural English** Listen and complete. Find one of the questions in tapescripts 7.7 and 7.8.

> **natural English**
> *When did you last ...?*
>
> **When did you last** _____ _____ ?
> = When was the last time you saw her?
> **When did you last** _____ _____ _____ ?
> a week ago / two years ago
> in December / last week
> a long time ago

7 Use the language in the **natural English** box. With a partner, ask and answer about these people:

your doctor   your dentist

your grandfather   your best friend

speaking it's your turn!

1 **Think!** Think about a teacher you had in the past.

> What was your teacher's name?
> What did he / she teach?
> How old were you?
> What was he / she like?
> What do you remember about him / her?
> When did you last see him / her?

2 Ask three people about their teacher. How many people liked their teacher?

> What was your teacher's name?

> **can you remember ...**
> ... six more object pronouns?
> He works near *me* / _____
> / _____ / _____ / _____
> / _____ / _____ .

extended speaking
people from your past

you're going to:

collect ideas	prepare an interview	tell a story	writing
read and answer questions about old friends	interview a partner about their friend	tell your partner's story	write your story

 ## collect ideas

1 With a partner, describe the people in the picture.

FACES FROM THE PAST
Long-distance love

I met Oliver when I was on a business trip two years ago. He was tall and dark, and he was quite good-looking. I liked him because he was really funny and he was also very clever. He lived in Brussels and I lived in Amsterdam, but I went out with him for about six months. I hate driving, but I went to Brussels most weekends. We went to the cinema a lot, and he took me to some great restaurants, but often we stayed at his place and watched old, romantic films. Then he got a new job, in Munich, and we stopped seeing each other. I wasn't heartbroken, but it was quite sad. I never saw him again, but a friend told me he got married last year.

Isabel Van Praag

2 Read the magazine letter. Complete the sentence.

Oliver was Isabel's _____ .

3 Match the question halves, then answer them with a partner.

When did she	she see him again?
Where did they	he like?
What was	meet Oliver?
How long did	stop seeing him?
Why did she	meet?
Did	she go out with him?

 ## prepare an interview

4 **Think!** Think of a person from your past that you <u>don't</u> see now.

examples a friend
an ex-boyfriend / girlfriend

Tell your partner the name.

> Marco – an old friend

5 **Think!** Write questions to ask your partner about their person, using the table.

possible questions

When / Where ... meet him / her?
What ... he / she like?
Where ... live?
What ... do together?
How long ... him / her?
When ... last see him / her?
Why ... stop seeing him / her?

 ## interview

6 Interview your partner. Remember the answers.

7 Now tell your partner <u>their</u> story.

You met Ana when you were at school ten years ago. She was ...

 ## tell a story

8 Find a new partner. Tell him / her your other partner's story.

 ## writing

9 Write about <u>your</u> friend for the 'Faces from the Past' page. Use the model in **exercise 1** and the questions in **exercise 5** to help you.

seven review

vocabulary appearance

1 Complete the dialogue about the pictures. Then practise with a partner.

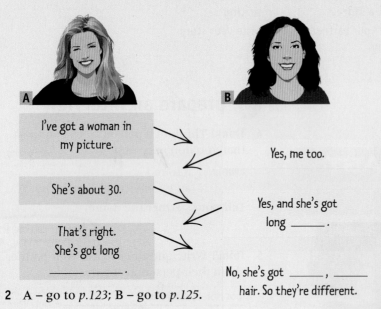

A I've got a woman in my picture.

Yes, me too.

She's about 30.

Yes, and she's got long _____.

That's right. She's got long _____ _____.

No, she's got _____, _____ hair. So they're different.

2 A – go to *p.123*; B – go to *p.125*.

vocabulary life story

1 **Think!** Use the questions to write about someone in your family.

Where / When was he / she born?

Where did he / she grow up?

When did he / she leave school?

What did he / she do (become) after school?

Where did he / she work?

When did he / she get married?

How many children has he / she got?

What does he / she do now?

example My father, Silvio, was born in Ravenna in 1958. He ...

2 Work with a partner. Read their text. Ask more questions:

What did he study at university? Where does he live now?

natural English

1 Order the words.

1 I / school / left / then / and / job / a / got

2 quite / sister / got / hair / my / has / long

3 girlfriend / your / you / did / see / when / last?

4 like / your / is / teacher / what?

5 hair / my / has got / brother / very / and / tall / is / brown

6 I / in / Italy / worked / after / and / that / went / Spain / to

2 Check your answers using the **natural English** boxes in unit seven.

test yourself!

Now cover the REVIEW section and test yourself on unit seven.

test your vocabulary

From this unit:

1 complete the descriptions:
   *He's sh _ _ _ and very
   at _ _ _ _ _ _ _ _.
   He's got a be _ _ _ and a
   mo _ _ _ _ _ _ _.
   She's got me _ _ _ _-length
   bl _ _ _ _ _ hair.
   She's quite th _ _ and very
   be _ _ _ _ _ _ _.*

2 write the opposite of: *funny,
   boring, hard-working, horrible,
   stupid*

3 write a verb in the past simple:
   *I _____ born in Liverpool and I
   _____ up there.
   She _____ married two years ago
   and she _____ a baby last year.*

   score [17]

gap-fill

Fill the gaps.

1 Why _____ he move to Rome in
   2003?

2 She left school in 2004, and
   _____ that, she got a job.

3 **A** What _____ your teacher like?
   B She's lovely.

4 She _____ do her homework
   because she was lazy.

   score [4]

error correction

Correct the errors.

1 When did she became a teacher?

2 He doesn't like she.

3 I not go out last night.

4 When you last see him?

   score [4]

   total score [25]

Look back at the unit contents on
p.55. Tick ✓ the language you can
use.

reading
I got lost!

lead-in

1 Stand up. Ask three people. Do you sometimes get lost:

in your town / city?   when you're on holiday?   on public transport?

2 (8.1) Listen to Lynne. Where did she get lost? Why?

vocabulary getting around

1 Complete the list with the verbs from the box.

~~ask for~~   see   give   get on   take   forget   understand   ask for   get off

Why do people get lost ?

⇨ they don't *ask for* directions
⇨ they _____ directions but don't _____ them
⇨ they forget to _____ a map
⇨ they _____ the wrong train
⇨ they _____ at the wrong station
⇨ people _____ them the wrong directions
⇨ they _____ the way
⇨ it's dark and they can't _____ the road signs

2 Match the pictures with the sentences in **exercise 1**.

3 Which sentences are true for you: always, sometimes, or never?

example   I sometimes forget to take a map when I go on holiday.

4 **8.2** **natural English** Listen. Do you hear the words in (brackets)?

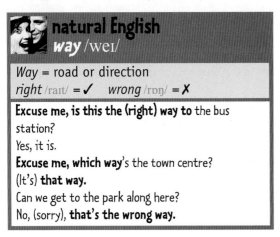

natural English
way /weɪ/

Way = road or direction
right /raɪt/ = ✓   *wrong* /rɒŋ/ = ✗

Excuse me, is this the (right) way to the bus station?
Yes, it is.
Excuse me, which way's the town centre?
(It's) **that way.**
Can we get to the park along here?
No, (sorry), **that's the wrong way.**

5 **pronunciation** Listen again and repeat. Copy the intonation.

6 Think of five places near your school. Ask your partner, like this:

Which way's the station?
Thanks.
It's that way.

read on

1 Read the stories. Tick ✓ <u>two</u> correct answers for each question.

  1 The Thompsons got lost because ... .
    a ☐ they didn't have a map.
    b ☐ they forgot the way.
    c ☐ they didn't ask for directions.

  2 The student got lost because ... .
    a ☐ he didn't ask for directions.
    b ☐ his pronunciation was bad.
    c ☐ a man gave him directions to the wrong city.

2 Read the Paris article again. Number the places on the map in the order the Thompsons visited them.

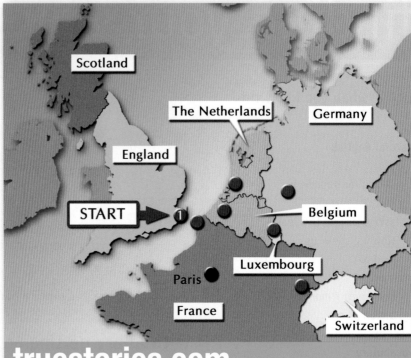

truestories.com

Excuse me, where's Paris?

In 1998, Martin and Lucy Thompson decided to drive from Dover, England, to Paris to spend a few days there with some friends. It was a long drive, so they took quite a lot of food and drink for the **journey**, but unfortunately, they forgot to take a map.

They got off the boat in Calais, France and immediately got lost, but they continued driving and didn't stop to ask for directions. When they got near the **border** with Switzerland, they knew it was the wrong road. They went back, this time driving through Luxembourg, then to Brussels. Many hours later, they got to Rotterdam in the Netherlands, and then finally arrived in Bonn, Germany, with no money, food, drink, or petrol. Some kind people gave them some money and they got back to Dover a week later, after driving more than 1500 kilometres.

Excuse me, where's Bath?

In 2002, a **foreign** student arrived at Heathrow Airport, London, on his way to study English at a language school in Bath, 175 km west of London. He didn't speak very much English, but he knew the question, 'Excuse me, how do I get to Bath?' He asked a lot of people for directions, but they didn't understand his accent. Finally, a nice man took him to the station and helped him get a train. The ticket was very expensive, so he didn't have any money or food for the journey, and only a small bottle of water. Six hours and 667 kilometres later, feeling very **hungry** and **thirsty,** he arrived in Perth, Scotland. He showed a woman a letter with the address of the language school. 'This isn't Bath, it's Perth!' she said. She took the student home, gave him a bed for the night, then paid for his ticket to Bath the next day.

glossary

journey (n) /ˈdʒɜːni/ when you travel from one place to another
border (n) /ˈbɔːdə/ official line between two countries
foreign (adj) /ˈfɒrən/ a foreign person is from a different country, not yours
hungry (adj) /ˈhʌŋgri/ if you're hungry, you want to eat something
thirsty (adj) /ˈθɜːsti/ if you're thirsty, you want to drink something

grammar *how much / many?*

1 Can you remember ...

five countable nouns? *example* apple

five uncountable nouns? *example* water

2 Complete the table with words from the box. Compare with a partner.

not many   a lot   quite   none /nʌn/

---

countable e.g. houses, people

How many books did you take on holiday?

none _____ _____ a lot

uncountable e.g. butter, rice

How much money did you take on holiday?

_____ not much _____ a lot   a lot

---

3 Work in A / B pairs. A – do the exercise below. B – go to *p.123.*

Student A Work with another A student. Circle *much* or *many.*

1 How much / many days did the Thompsons want to spend in Paris?

2 How much / many people did the Thompsons ask for directions?

3 How much / many food and drink did they take with them?

4 How much / many countries did they go to?

5 How much / many kilometres did they drive?

6 How much / many petrol did they have in Bonn?

4 Answer your questions with *none, not much / many, quite a lot,* or *a lot.* Read the article again if necessary.

5 As – find a B partner. Read your questions to your new partner. Can they answer?

go to **language reference** *and* **practice exercises** *p.138*

speaking *it's your turn!*

1 With a partner, write a questionnaire about people's habits, using *how much* and *how many.* Use the verbs in the box. Write your questions in the questionnaire.

buy   eat   drink   read   drive   go to   see
meet   watch   have   have got   *your own ideas*

LIFESTYLE QUESTIONNAIRE

	STUDENT 1	STUDENT 2
How many holidays do you have every year?		
How much wine do you drink every day?		
How many magazines do you read every week?		
1		
2		
3		
4		
5		

2 Interview two people. Complete the questionnaire.

Sergio, how many CDs do you buy every month?

Well, not many, but at Christmas, I buy a lot for my friends.

3 Find your first partner. Tell them about the two students you interviewed.

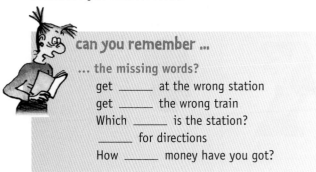

can you remember ...

... the missing words?

get _____ at the wrong station

get _____ the wrong train

Which _____ is the station?

_____ for directions

How _____ money have you got?

wordb

prepositions of place

Look at the map, then complete the sentence below
with words from the box.

behind /bɪˈhaɪnd/	at the end	next to
on	between /bɪˈtwiːn/	in
opposite /ˈɒpəzɪt/	in front of /ɪnˈfrʌntəv/	near

The hotel's _____ the bank.

The bank's _____ the cinema.

The cinema's _____ the shop and the café.

The car park's _____ the hotel.

The hotel's _____ the church.

The statue's _____ the park.

The lake's _____ the park.

The boat's _____ the lake.

The park's _____ of the road.

test your partner

– Where's the lake?

– It's in the park.

– That's right.

me and *go*; *bring* and *take*

e the verbs in the gaps.

bring go take come

_____ over here.

_____ over there.

_____ my glasses here, please.

_____ this to the kitchen.

2 **8.3** **Work in two groups, A and B. Close your books. Listen and follow the instructions.**

3 **Work with a partner. Write *come*, *go*, *bring*, or *take*. Then listen again to check your answers.**

OK, everybody, now, ¹ _____ here and stand next to the tape recorder, and ² _____ your English coursebook with you.

Now, A students, ³ _____ to the door, and ⁴ _____ your books with you.

Right, now B students, ⁵ _____ back to your chairs and ⁶ _____ your books with you. Then ⁷ _____ here again, and this time, ⁸ _____ your pen.

A students, ⁹ _____ back to your chairs and sit down. Don't ¹⁰ _____ your books – put them near the door.

B students, ¹¹ _____ to the door, pick up a book, then ¹² _____ it to the correct A student. Then ¹³ _____ to your chair and sit down.

listening
how to ... get around a building

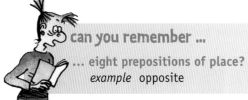 **can you remember ...**

... eight prepositions of place?
example opposite

grammar *there is / are*

1 Look round your classroom. Tell a partner what you can see.

example I can see five chairs next to the window.

2 Don't look round the classroom! Underline the correct answers .

1 There's a / There isn't a clock on the wall.

2 There's a / There isn't a photocopier behind me.

3 There's some / There isn't any paper on the teacher's table.

4 There's some / There isn't any food in the room.

5 There are some / There aren't any pictures on the wall.

6 There are some / There aren't any dictionaries in the room.

Now look up. Say the correct sentences with a partner.

3 Complete the table. Use the sentences in **exercise 2** to help you.

NOUNS	POSITIVE	NEGATIVE
SINGULAR	There's a table.	There isn't a table.
UNCOUNTABLE	There ___ some food.	There ___ ___ food.
PLURAL	There ___ some chairs.	There ___ ___ chairs.

NOUNS	QUESTIONS	SHORT ANSWERS
SINGULAR	Is there a table?	Yes, there is.
UNCOUNTABLE	___ ___ ___ food?	No, there ___ .
PLURAL	___ ___ ___ chairs?	Yes, there ___ .

4 (**8.4**) **pronunciation** Listen and check your answers. Listen again and practise linking the words.

examples there's a   there isn't any   there are

5 **Think!** Write five questions about your classroom.

examples Is there a TV in the room? Are there any videos or DVDs?
Ask and answer with a partner.

go to **language reference** *and* **practice exercises** *p.139*

listen to this

tune in

1 Look at the floor plan of the school. Is your school similar or different?

Second Floor

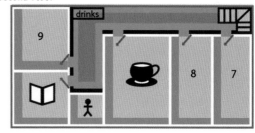

First Floor

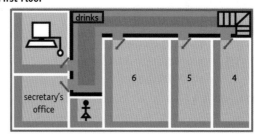

Ground Floor

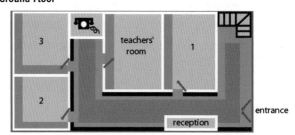

2 (**8.5**) **natural English** Listen and complete. Then practise with a partner.

natural English
asking for directions

Excuse me. Where's the coffee bar?

It's ____ ____ ____ floor.

Excuse me. Is there a photocopier ____ ____

____ ?

Yes, in the library.

Excuse me. Is there a lift here?

No, I'm sorry, ____ ____ .

listen carefully

3 **8.6** Listen and answer the questions.

1 Is the man happy at the end of the first conversation? Why / Why not?

2 Is the student happy at the end of the second conversation? Why / Why not?

4 Listen again. Answer TRUE or FALSE.

conversation 1

1 You can buy fruit in the coffee bar.

2 There isn't any hot food.

3 It closes in an hour.

conversation 2

4 The student can use the photocopier in the library at the moment.

5 He can use the photocopier in the teachers' room.

6 He wants two copies of a homework exercise.

listening challenge

5 **8.7** Read the summary. Listen and correct four mistakes in the information.

The woman wants the lift because she has to take some videos to the teachers' room. The receptionist gives her directions – go upstairs to the first floor, along the corridor, turn right, and the library is the second door on the right. She thanks the receptionist.

listen again with the **tapescript** *p.151–152*

6 **natural English** Read the box. Circle the examples of *well* in tapescripts 8.6 and 8.7. How do you say *well* in your language?

natural English
well

We use *well* a lot in spoken English, often when we are beginning an answer.

A Is the library this way?
B **Well**, it is, but it's closed at the moment.

vocabulary directions

1 Match the phrases and diagrams. Then practise the phrases, stressing the <u>underlined</u> words.

go upstairs	it's at the <u>end</u> of the <u>corridor</u>	turn <u>left</u>
go downstairs	it's the <u>first</u> door on your <u>left</u>	turn <u>right</u>
go along the <u>corridor</u>	it's the <u>second</u> door on your <u>right</u>	

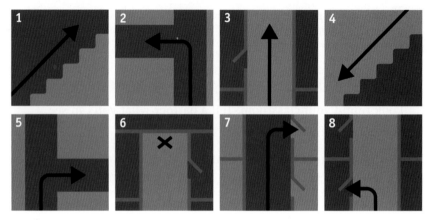

2 Work in A / B pairs. You are in reception. Use the floor plan on *p.67* to give directions.

A – ask B directions to:

– computer room   – coffee bar   – toilets   – office

B – ask A directions to:

– drinks machine   – library   – teachers' room   – phone

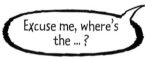
Excuse me, where's the ... ?

Go downstairs, along ...

writing

1 **Think!** Think of two places / things in <u>your</u> school.

examples library   drinks machine

Write directions to these places from your classroom. Don't write the name of the place.

> 1 Go to the door, turn left, go along the corridor, go downstairs, and it's on your right. WHERE ARE YOU?

2 Give your directions to different people. Can they answer the question?

can you remember ...

... the missing words?

go upstairs / go _____
turn left / turn _____
go _____ the corridor
it's the second door _____ your right
Is there a toilet on this _____ ?

help with pronunciation and listening

pronunciation sounds /ʃ/, /tʃ/, and /dʒ/

1 **Listen and repeat the sounds 8.8 and phrases.**

/ʃ/ a Poli<u>sh</u> dic<u>t</u>ionary

/tʃ/ a Fren<u>ch</u> pic<u>t</u>ure

/dʒ/ the <u>G</u>erman langua<u>g</u>e

2 **Work with a partner. Say the words in the box, and put them in the correct columns in the table.**

dangerous	teacher	orange	bridge	sausages
China	church	station	Russia	fish
chips	journalist	cheap	Belgium	sugar
chef	sure	chocolate		

	/ʃ/	/tʃ/	/dʒ/
nationalities	Polish	French	German
food you cook			
sweet things you eat			
things in a town			
countries			
jobs			
adjectives			

3 **Listen and check.**
8.9

listening prediction (2)

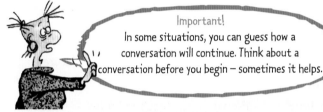

Important!
In some situations, you can guess how a conversation will continue. Think about a conversation before you begin – sometimes it helps.

1 **Look at the pictures. What does the woman want?**

2 **Work with a partner. You phone Trainline to buy a ticket from London to Liverpool. In the table, tick ✓ the questions you think the person will ask you.**

questions	Trainline person asks you	answers
1 Which station are you travelling from?	✓	
2 What time is my train?		
3 When do you want to travel?		
4 Can I pay by credit card?		
5 Do you want a single or return?		
6 What time of day do you want to leave?		
7 How much is the ticket?		
8 Is it just one ticket?		
9 How would you like to pay?		

3 **Listen. Which questions in exercise 2 does the 8.10 Trainline person ask?**

4 **Listen again. Write the answers in the table.**

*listen again with the **tapescript** p.152*

5 **natural English Listen and notice the <u>underlined</u> 8.11 stress. Practise the dialogues with a partner.**

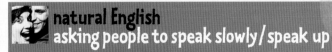

natural English
asking people to speak slowly / speak up

| Sorry, could you <u>speak slowly</u>, please? | Yes, sure. |
| Could you <u>speak up</u>, please? | Yes, of course. |

eight review

grammar *how much / many?*

1 Write seven questions. Use a phrase from each column.

example How much coffee did you drink yesterday?

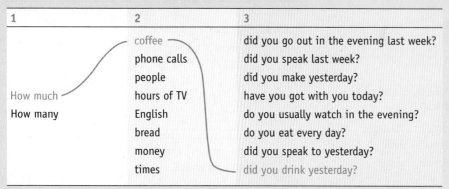

1	2	3
	coffee	did you go out in the evening last week?
	phone calls	did you speak last week?
	people	did you make yesterday?
How much	hours of TV	have you got with you today?
How many	English	do you usually watch in the evening?
	bread	do you eat every day?
	money	did you speak to yesterday?
	times	did you drink yesterday?

2 Ask and answer the questions with a partner. You can use these phrases:

a lot   quite a lot   not much / not many   none   about (four or five, etc.)

vocabulary directions

go to **pairwork** *p.124*

grammar *there is / are*

1 With a partner, write eight sentences about the town you are in. Use the words in the box. Make some sentences true and some false.

examples There's a cathedral. (true)
There aren't any bridges in the centre. (false – there are two)
There are two big squares. (false – there's only one)

church	fountain	castle	university	bridge	cathedral	museum
palace	factory	market	square	beach	gym	hotel
language school		Chinese restaurant		Italian restaurant		*your own ideas*

2 Read your sentences to a new partner. They say if they are true or false.

🎭 natural English

1 Complete the conversations.

1 A _____ me, is this the way _____ the station?
   B I'm sorry, I can't hear you. Could you _____ up, _____?
   A Yes, of _____. I said, 'Is this the way _____ the station?'
   B Oh, no, it isn't. It's that _____.
   A Thanks a lot.

2 A _____ me, is _____ a toilet here?
   B Yes, it's on the first _____.

2 Check your answers using the **natural English** boxes in unit eight.

Now cover the REVIEW section and test yourself on unit eight.

test your vocabulary

From this unit, write down:

1 the missing word: _____ *for directions; forget to* _____ *a map;* _____ *on the wrong bus; get* _____ *at the wrong station*

2 the directions in order:
right / door / second / the / on / the / it's
of / the / at / corridor / end / the / it's
upstairs / along / go / the / and / corridor
downstairs / turn / go / right / and

3 possible prepositions for this gap:
The car park is b _ _ _ _ _ _/
n _ _ _ / o _ _ _ _ _ _ _ _/
n _ _ _ t_ / _n f _ _ _ _
o _ the station.

score ☐ 12

gap-fill

Fill the gaps.

1 _____ me. Where's the coffee bar?
2 **A** Is this the _____ to the station?
  B Yes, it is.
3 Is _____ a lift here?
4 Sorry, I don't understand. Could you speak _____, please?

score ☐ 4

error correction

Correct the errors.

1 Come here and take your book with you.
2 How many money have you got?
3 I think there is two tables in room four.
4 **A** Is there a food?
  B No, there isn't.

score ☐ 4

total score ☐ 20

Look back at the unit contents on *p.63.* Tick ✓ the language you can use.

reading backpacking

lead-in

Think! Think of three countries you would like to visit. Why do you want to go there? Where would you like to stay? Ask a partner.

grammar *have to / don't have to / do I have to ...?; can / can't* (permission)

1   Match pictures a to f with sentences 1 to 6.

   1   You have to **clean your room**.
   2   You have to **pay the bill** when you leave.
   3   You can **sleep** until 9.00 a.m.
   4   You have to **cook your breakfast**.
   5   You have to **show your passport / ID card** when you arrive at a hotel abroad.
   6   You can **use the minibar**.

2   In a hotel, two sentences in **exercise 1** are not true. Which two? Why?

3   Tick ✓ the correct answer.

   Have to /ˈhæftə/ means:

   a   it's possible ☐   b   it's a good idea ☐   c   it's necessary ☐

4   Answer the questions.

   1   Are these sentences true?
      You *don't have to* clean your room in a hotel.
      You *don't have to* cook your breakfast in a hotel.

   2   Tick ✓ the correct answer.
      Don't have to means:
      a   it's not possible ☐   b   it's not necessary ☐   c   it's not a good idea ☐

5 Complete the table. Compare with a partner.

POSITIVE			NEGATIVE			
I / You / We / They	have to	go.	I / You / We / They	_____	have to	go.
He / She / It	has to		He / She / It	_____		
QUESTIONS			**SHORT ANSWERS**			
_____ you	have to	go?	Yes, you do. / No, you _____ .			
_____ she			Yes, she _____ . / No, she _____ .			

6 Write *have to* or *don't have to*.

> In most hotels ...
>
> 1 you _____ eat dinner.
> 2 you _____ pay for drinks from the minibar.
> 3 you _____ get up at 7.30.
> 4 you _____ pay when you arrive.
> 5 you _____ stay a minimum of two nights.
> 6 you _____ give your key to reception when you leave.

7 With a partner, ask and answer about **exercise 6**, like this:

A Do you have to eat dinner in a hotel?

B No, you don't.

go to **language reference** *and* **practice exercises** *p.139*

read on

1 What are *backpackers* and *youth hostels* /juːθ ˈhɒstlz/? Tell a partner.

2 Read the FAQs (Frequently Asked Questions) about youth hostels. What do you think the answers are? Tell your partner.

youth hostels: FAQs

1 Do I have to sleep in a room with other people?

2 Do I have to bring anything? (e.g. **a sleeping bag**)

3 Do I have to clean my room?

4 Can I cook my breakfast or dinner?

5 Can I **book** a room in a youth hostel **in advance**?

6 Can I arrive at a youth hostel at any time?

7 Are youth hostels only for young people?

8 Do I have to be a **member** to stay in a youth hostel?

> **glossary**
>
> **sleeping bag** (n) a warm bag for sleeping in when camping
> **book (in advance)** (v) ask to have a hotel room / table in a restaurant before you go
> **member** (n) person who is a part of a group / organisation (you often pay to be a member)

3 Work in A / B pairs.
A – read the information on *p.73*.
B – read the information on *p.124*.

Which questions in **exercise 2** can you answer now?

4 Ask your partner the questions in **exercise 2** you can't answer.

5 **natural English** Read the box, then find more examples in the two articles.

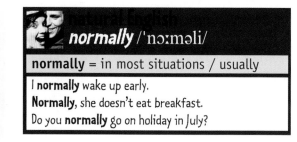

> **natural English**
>
> ***normally*** /ˈnɔːməli/
>
> **normally** = in most situations / usually
>
> I **normally** wake up early.
> **Normally**, she doesn't eat breakfast.
> Do you **normally** go on holiday in July?

6 Tell a partner three things you *normally do / don't normally do* on holiday.

example I normally go to the gym.
Normally, I don't get up early.

7 Find someone who has stayed in a youth hostel. Ask them about it.

Where was it?   Who did you go with?

Milly

Youth hostels
Frequently Asked Questions

Do I have to bring anything?

Usually you don't have to bring things for the bed, but there are some places where you have to bring sheets or a sleeping bag, and normally you have to bring your own towels and anything you **need** for washing.

Can I cook breakfast or dinner?

Most hostels have a kitchen where you can do some cooking. Sometimes you have to bring **equipment** with you, and you have to clean the kitchen when you finish cooking.

Can I arrive at a youth hostel at any time?

Most large city hostels are open 24 hours a day, but others close at certain times during the day and night. Normally, you can check in or out between 7.00-10.00 and 17.00-22.30.

Do I have to be a member to stay in a youth hostel?

No. Non-members can stay in some hostels but they pay a bit more.

> glossary
>
> **need** (v) if you need sth, you want or have to have it
>
> **equipment** (n) /ɪˈkwɪpmənt/ things you need for an activity, e.g. for cooking

writing

1 Milly stayed at the Arpacay Hostel in the Czech Republic. Read the advert and e-mail she sent to her family on the second morning. Does she like it? Complete the e-mail.

> **Arpacay Hostel**
> A. Jenstejnska 1, Prague 2
>
> Are you looking for a clean and comfortable private room with breakfast for $12? It is easy to get here from the airport and we are only 15 minutes from the famous Charles Bridge. A terrace with a beautiful view, laundry, 24H free Internet access, and friendly staff.

> Hi everyone
>
> I'm now at the Arpacay Hostel in Prague. It's very ¹ _____ (only $12 a night), but my room is clean and ² _____ , the people who work here are ³ _____ , and there are fantastic ⁴ _____ from the terrace at the top of the building.
> I can use the ⁵ _____ here as well – and I don't have to pay!
> Last night I ⁶ _____ to Charles Bridge, which is very near the hostel, and today I want to visit Prague Castle.
> Love
> Milly

2 Go to *p.124*.

speaking it's your turn!

1 Work with a partner. Complete this Internet guide for your 'perfect' youth hostel.

> ## the perfect hostel.com
>
> **Come and stay with us in the perfect youth hostel. Why is it perfect? This is why.**
>
> You can *book rooms online*.　　You don't have to *cook your breakfast*.
> You can _____ .　　You don't have to _____ .
> You can _____ .　　You don't have to _____ .
> You can _____ .　　You don't have to _____ .

2 Talk to other pairs. Tell them about your 'perfect' hostel. Which hostel is best, and why?

> In my perfect hostel, you can ...

can you remember ...

... the correct forms of *have to*?

You _____ have to do it.　_____ he have to go?
She _____ to go now.　I _____ have to work today.
Do you _____ to pay?　He _____ have to do it.

wordbooster

numbers (2)

1 **9.1** Listen and complete the numbers. What are the totals for the restaurant and the supermarket?

Banco Union

4924 _ _ _ _ 3721 _ _ _ _
expiry date 12 / _ _
P ALMEIDA

MasterCard

Hill Finders Hostel

single room	£25
2–6 bed dorm	£16 per person
family room (up to 4)	___
breakfast extra	___ per person

3-night stay: 10% less for all rooms. No deposit necessary.

tel 01732 556 424
for further information

PIECE OF PIZZA!

1 Pizza Napoletana	€7.50
1 Spaghetti Carbonara	___
2 glasses of red wine	€5.60
2 coffees	€3.50
SUBTOTAL	___
service @ 10%	___
TOTAL	___

SCALA supermarket

tea	£1.60
butter	___
tomatoes	___
apples	£1.40
ice cream	£2.90
TOTAL	___

2 Work with a partner. Say a number / amount. Your partner says what it is.

test your partner
– Three euros fifty?
– That's right.
– That's two coffees at Piece of Pizza.

money

1 Work in A pairs and B pairs. Answer your questions, using the information from numbers (2).

A pairs (credit card and restaurant)
1 What's the last number on the **credit card**?
2 What's the total restaurant **bill**?
3 You **pay the** restaurant **bill** with €30. How much **change** do you get?
4 You went to the restaurant with a friend. You both had Spaghetti Carbonara and a glass of red wine. With **service**, how much did the meal **cost**?
5 You **share** the **bill**. How much did each person **pay**?

B pairs (hostel and supermarket)
1 Do you have to **pay a deposit** at the hostel?
2 A friend stayed in a single room for three nights. How much did it **cost**? How much did he **save**?
3 When the person went to Scala supermarket, did she **buy** any potatoes?
4 Do Scala **sell** fruit?
5 You stayed in a single room in the hostel for one night (with breakfast), then went out and **bought** some ice cream at Scala. How much did you **spend**?

2 As – work with a B partner. Ask your questions. Can your partner answer?

listening
how to ... book a room

vocabulary hotels

1 Look at the brochure. Answer the questions. Compare with a partner.

holiday palace hotel
Christchurch | New Zealand

Room Price Guide (breakfast extra)
single room US$116 | double room US$141

FREE Parking

1 Is the room a **single room**, a **double** /dʌbl/ **room**, or a **twin**?
2 Is the room **en-suite** /ɒnˈswiːt/?
3 Has it got a **bath** /bɑːθ/ and a **shower** /ˈʃaʊə/?
4 Has it got **Internet access** /ˈækses/?
5 Has the hotel got **parking**?
6 Is there a **swimming pool** and a **gym** /dʒɪm/?
7 Has it got a **restaurant**?
8 Is breakfast **included** in the **price**?

2 Look at the brochure again. Then close your book. Tell your partner what you can remember.

You can see ...   The hotel has got ...   There's ...

3 **Think!** Think about a hotel you know. What's it like? What has it got? Make notes. Use the questions in **exercise 1** to help you.

4 **9.2** **natural English** Read the box and listen. How many times do you hear ... ?

I think so ☐   I don't think so ☐

> ### I (don't) think so
>
> Has the hotel got a bar?
> Yes, **I think so.** (= you're 70–95% sure it has)
> Is there a pool?
> No, **I don't think so.** (= you're 70–95% sure it hasn't)

5 Ask your partner about the hotel they know. If they aren't sure, they can say, 'I think so / I don't think so'.

listen to this

tune in

1 **9.3** Stephen phones a hotel for information. Listen to the beginning of the conversation. Tick ✓ the phrases in pink you hear.

☐ I'd like some information, please.
☐ Could you give me some information, please?

☐ Yes, sure.
☐ Yes, of course.

☐ How much is a double room?
☐ What's the price of a double room?

listen carefully

2 Match 1 to 4 with a to d to make more questions Stephen can ask.

1	Is breakfast	a	parking?
2	Have you got	b	included?
3	Do I have to pay	c	pool?
4	Is there a	d	a deposit?

3 Listen. What are the answers?

listening challenge

4 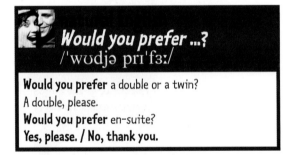 Stephen decides to book a room. With a partner, write four questions the receptionist will ask.

example What date would you like to come?

Remember – it helps if you can predict the conversation.

5 Listen. Do you hear your questions? Do you hear other questions? Listen again for the answers.

listen again with the **tapescript** *p.152*

6 natural English **pronunciation** Read and listen. What's the pronunciation of *Would you prefer?* Practise the dialogue with a partner.

Would you prefer ...?
/ˈwʊdjə prɪˈfɜː/

Would you prefer a double or a twin?
A double, please.
Would you prefer en-suite?
Yes, please. / No, thank you.

---

7 Work with a partner. You are in the hotel bar. Practise the first dialogue, then practise again with the prompts.

example something to drink / tea or coffee

A Would you like something to drink?
B Yes, please.
A Would you prefer tea or coffee?
B Coffee, please.

a glass of wine / red or white
a sandwich / ham or cheese
coffee / black or white

speaking it's your turn!

1 Work in two groups – As and Bs. Prepare your part of the conversation below. Don't write anything.

As – you are receptionists.
Bs – you are callers.

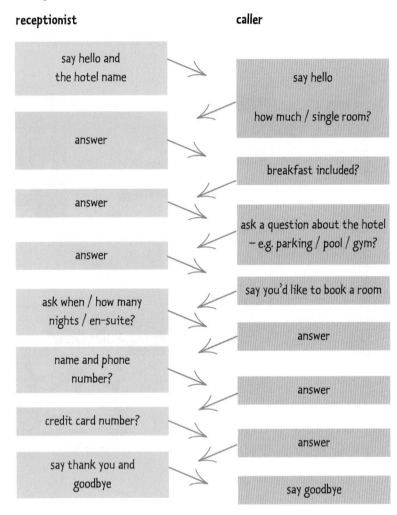

receptionist — caller

- say hello and the hotel name → say hello
- how much / single room?
- answer → breakfast included?
- answer → ask a question about the hotel – e.g. parking / pool / gym?
- answer → say you'd like to book a room
- ask when / how many nights / en-suite? → answer
- name and phone number? → answer
- credit card number? → answer
- say thank you and goodbye → say goodbye

2 As – find a B partner. Practise your conversation together.

3 **Think!** Change roles. As – you are callers. Bs – you are receptionists. Think about your part of the conversation. Then practise it together.

can you remember ...

... the missing words?
Do I _____ to pay a deposit?
Is breakfast _____ ?
She _____ to go now.
I think _____ . / I don't _____ _____ .
Would you _____ a double or a twin room?

extended speaking
my kind of hotel

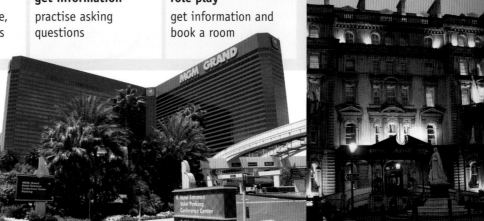

collect ideas

1 **Think!** Think about your answers.

– When did you last stay in a hotel?

– Where was it?

– Why were you there?

– Did you like it?

Tell a partner.

invent a hotel

2 **Think!** You are the manager of a hotel. Think about the table below. Don't write anything.

What's the hotel called?   Where is it?

What facilities have you got ?   What are the prices?

_____ Hotel   in _____ (town / city / country)

room facilities
(e.g. TV in every room)   _____
     _____

hotel facilities
(e.g. pool)   _____
     _____

prices

single room	_____ per night
double / twin room	_____ per night
breakfast included? if not, price?	_____
dinner included? if not, price of set dinner?	_____
credit cards accepted?	yes ☐ no ☐
deposit?	yes ☐ (how much? _____) no ☐

3 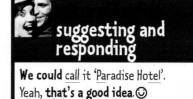 **natural English pronunciation**
9.6 Listen and notice the underlined stress. Practise the dialogues with a partner.

suggesting and responding

We could call it 'Paradise Hotel'.
Yeah, **that's a good idea.** ☺
Let's have a French restaurant.
Hmm. **I'm not sure about that.** ☹

4 With a partner, compare your ideas for a hotel. Use the phrases in the **natural English** box.

5 Complete the table using the best ideas.

6 With your partner, write the questions you need to get information about your hotel.

    example   What's the hotel called?
                  Is there parking?

role play

7 Find a new partner.

  A – you are a hotel receptionist. Go to *p.125*.

  B – you'd like to stay at A's hotel. Go to *p.127*.

8 Change roles. Complete the other form, and repeat the role play.

9 Which hotel do you prefer? Why?

nine review

grammar *have to / don't have to / do I have to ...?*

1 Work with a partner. Look at the table. You have three minutes to write as many sentences as possible, beginning:

Alex has to ... but he doesn't have to ...

Simone has to ... but she doesn't have to ...

They both have to ...

Alex has to wash up, but he doesn't have to clean the flat.

Alex		Simone
wash up		clean the flat
go to the supermarket		make the dinner
make the breakfast		make the breakfast
wash the car		feed the cat
go to work		go to work
pay the bills		pay the bills

2 A – shut your book. B – ask A questions. Then swap.

example **B** Who has to go to the supermarket?
   A Alex.

vocabulary money and numbers

1 Complete each sentence with a word / phrase on the right.

1	I bought	a	cost?
2	Do you have to pay a	b	card?
3	Have you got a credit	c	€50.
4	What's the expiry	d	deposit?
5	Is service	e	date?
6	I paid	f	bill?
7	How much did the book	g	two CDs.
8	Did you pay the	h	included?

2 Read your sentences to a partner. Are they the same?

natural English

1 Correct the two errors in each line. Then compare with a partner.

1 **A** Let's to go out this evening. **B** Yes, it's a good idea.
2 **A** Is the hotel got a restaurant? **B** Mmm. I'm not sure for that.
3 **A** Does it normal rain there in July? **B** No, I no think so.
4 **A** Would you prefer to a double room? **B** Please, yes.

2 Check your answers using the **natural English** boxes in unit nine. Then practise the correct dialogues with your partner.

test yourself!

Now cover the REVIEW section and test yourself on unit nine.

test your vocabulary

From this unit, write down:

1 these numbers in words:
   16; £7.50; 10%;
   073246 (telephone number)
   example $10 = ten dollars
2 four more 'money' verbs: *pay*, ...
3 words to complete these phrases:
   a double _____ ; *pay the* _____ ;
   pay by credit _____ ; *Is service*
   _____ ?

score 12

gap-fill

Fill the gaps.

1 **A** _____ you prefer tea or coffee?
   B Coffee, please.
2 **A** Do you _____ to book in
      advance at that restaurant?
   B No, I _____ think so.
3 **A** _____ go out this evening.
   B That's a good idea.

score 4

error correction

Correct the errors.

1 Do normally you stay at home in
   the evening?
2 Robbie not have to work this
   Saturday.
3 **A** We could to paint the living
      room pink and green.
   B Hmm ... I'm not sure about that.
4 She have to get the bus at 7.30.

score 4

total score 20

Look back at the unit contents on *p.71.* Tick ✓ the language you can use.

tick ✓ when you know this

natural English
- [ ] talking about ages
- [ ] *quite / very well*
- [ ] giving opinions (2)
- [ ] offering help

grammar
- [ ] *can / can't* (ability)
- [ ] *something, anything, nothing,* etc.

vocabulary
- [ ] action verbs
- [ ] parts of the body
- [ ] common phrases

reading
babies

lead-in

1 **Think!** Think of a baby you know.

Who are the parents?   How old is he / she?

What's the baby called?   What's he / she like?

Tell a partner.

2 ⏺ **10.1** Listen to Olivia, and then Roger. What are their answers to **exercise 1**?

vocabulary action verbs

1 Match the verbs and pictures.

sleep	play (with something)	pick something up	smile	cry /kraɪ/
walk	throw /θrəʊ/ (something)	laugh /lɑːf/	crawl /krɔːl/	wave /weɪv/

2 **pronunciation** In **exercise 1**, find:

two verbs with the /aɪ/ sound (e.g. *write* /raɪt/)

two verbs with the /eɪ/ sound (e.g. *make* /meɪk/)

two verbs with the /ɔː/ sound (e.g. *talk* /tɔːk/)

test your partner

– *Crawl?*

– *That's right.*

79

read on

1 Complete the sentences with a partner. If you don't know, guess.

  1 Newborn (= new) babies sleep ——— hours a day.

  2 Babies understand 'no' when they are about ——— months old.

  3 Babies start to use 'baby talk' at about ——— months.

  4 They start to crawl at about ——— months.

2 Read the article and find the answers to exercise 1.

3 True or false?

  1 Babies know who you are between three and six months old.

  2 They can laugh when they are about three months old.

  3 They can wave goodbye before they are a year.

  4 When they are about eight months, they can see well.

  5 They can stand without help at nine months.

  6 They learn to eat with a spoon at ten to twelve months.

4 **natural English** Read the box. Find four similar examples in the article.

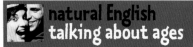

> **natural English**
> ## talking about ages
>
> Babies can smile:
> **at** about 4–6 weeks. NOT ~~with 4–6 weeks~~
> **when** they're about 4–6 weeks old.
> NOT when they ~~have~~ 4–6 weeks (old).

5 Can you answer the questions with a partner, using *at ...* or *when they are ...*?

At what age can children ...

walk?	write?
run?	dance?
speak quite well?	swim?
read?	wave?

Watch your baby grow!

AT 0–2 MONTHS

Babies can see from **birth**, but only about 20–30 cms – so they can see your face if you are near, but not very well. They have good **vision** when they are about eight months old. However, they can usually hear well by one month. At this age, they sleep about 15–16 hours a day. Babies cry from the start, but they develop two cries: one for 'I'm thirsty' and a different one for 'I'm tired'. They can usually smile at about four to six weeks.

AT 3–6 MONTHS

At about three months, they laugh and they start to **recognise** you. Babies at this age can hold their heads up when they're sitting. They begin to say baby words like 'coo' and 'ah-goo'. Typically, they play with their hands and feet, and they take things and put them in their mouths.

AT 7–9 MONTHS

By this stage, babies sleep a little less (about 14 hours), and they're beginning to crawl. Normally they can sit up without help and by the time they're nine months old, they can usually stand if they are holding onto a table or holding onto you.

AT 10–12 MONTHS

When babies are a year old, they can usually stand without help and they are beginning to walk. They can understand the word 'no', and they can also say 'mama' and 'dada' to the correct person. They start to pick up small things with one hand, which is important later for learning to eat with a **spoon**, write, and **draw**. They can throw things and wave goodbye.

grammar *can / can't* (ability)

1 Complete the table with *can* or *can't*. Compare with a partner.

CAN/CAN'T	
positive	negative
Babies _____ smile at 4–6 weeks.	They _____ walk at 6 months.
questions / short answers	
_____ they walk at 6 months?	Yes, they _____ . / No, they _____ .

2 Look at pictures 3 to 10 in **vocabulary exercise 1** on *p.79*. What can babies do at <u>six months</u>? Look at the text if necessary.

At six months, they can … They can't …

3 Work with a partner. Write six questions about babies at different ages. Use the text to help you.

example Can they stand at three months?

Find a new partner. Ask your questions. Can they answer?

4 **natural English** Put the sentences in order of ability from 1 to 4.

> **natural English**
> *quite / very well*
>
> I can swim **quite well**. ☐   I **can't** swim. ☐
> I **can't** swim **very well**. ☐   I can swim **very well**. ☐

5 Listen and check. Practise the sentences.

6 Tell a partner how well you can do the things in the pictures, using the phrases. Then tell your partner three other things you can / can't do very / quite well.

go to **language reference** *and* **practice exercises** *p.140*

speaking it's your turn!

1 Answer the quiz questions with a partner.

How much do you know about …?

Babies
Can babies swim at one year?

Children
Can children draw a circle when they're two?

Adults
Can adults run 5 kilometres in an hour?

Animals
Can cats stand on two legs?

2 (10.3) Listen. Were you right?

language reminder
*Can **babies** swim?* = all babies, babies in general
NOT *Can ~~the~~ babies swim?*

3 With your partner, write five quiz questions about people in your class.

examples Can Mario run five kilometres in an hour?
Can Lucy play the guitar?

4 Work with another pair. Ask your questions. Can they guess the correct answers?

Can Hiro sing well?

Yes, I think he can.

That's right.

can you remember …

… eight more action verbs from p.79?

example sleep

wordbooster

parts of the body

1 Label the pictures with words from the box.

chest	head	hand	hair	foot / feet (pl)
nose	mouth	ear	shoulder	back
eyes	tooth / teeth (pl)	stomach	toes	neck
arm	leg	fingers	thumb	

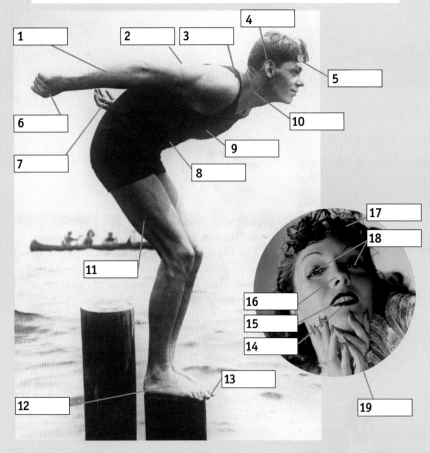

2 pronunciation Look at the underlined sounds. Is the pronunciation the same or different?

example b<u>a</u>ck / <u>a</u>rm – different   f<u>ee</u>t / t<u>ee</u>th – the same

1 st<u>o</u>mach / n<u>o</u>se   4 t<u>oe</u> / n<u>o</u>se
2 h<u>ea</u>d / <u>ea</u>r   5 f<u>oo</u>t / t<u>oo</u>th
3 thum<u>b</u> / <u>b</u>ack   6 sh<u>ou</u>lder / m<u>ou</u>th

3   **Listen and check. Practise the words.**

test your partner

– *Ear?*

– *That's right.*

common phrases

1 Complete the phrases below using words from the box. Compare with a partner.

lift	matter	terrible	fine	broke
look	kind	wrong	need	happened

1
A Do you _____ any help?
B No, thanks, I'm _____ .

2
A You don't _____ well.
B No, I feel _____ .

3
A What _____ ?
B I _____ my arm skiing.

4
A Can I **give you a** _____ ?
B Thanks, **that's very** _____ of you.

5
A What's the _____ ?
B **There's something** _____ **with** this drinks machine.

2 Practise the dialogues with a partner. Then close your books. Can you remember them?

listening

how to ... offer help

lead-in

1 Think! Read the questionnaire and think about your answers.

To help or not to help?

1 You're sitting opposite someone on a train. She doesn't look well. What do you do?
- a) say, 'Are you OK?' ☐
- b) say nothing and read your newspaper ☐

2 A man is at a bus stop on a cold night. There's no one in the street. You're in your car. What do you do?
- a) stop and say, 'Can I give you a lift?' ☐
- b) don't stop – continue driving ☐

3 A child (about 7-8) is standing in the street, crying. There isn't anyone with her. What do you do?
- a) say something, e.g. 'What's the matter?' ☐
- b) say nothing ☐

4 An old lady in front of you leaves the supermarket with two large shopping bags. She isn't with anyone. What do you do?
- a) say, 'Do you need any help?' ☐
- b) do nothing ☐

5 You're in your car on a quiet road. You see a man at the side of the road. There's something wrong with his car. What do you do?
- a) stop and say something, e.g. 'Is there anything I can do?' ☐
- b) do nothing ☐

2 **natural English** Listen and complete, then practise the sentences.

> **natural English**
> **giving opinions (2)**
>
> I think **it's better to** say something because (maybe) _____ _____ _____ .
> I think **it's better to** say nothing because (perhaps) _____ _____ _____ _____ _____ .

3 Talk about your answers to the questionnaire in small groups. Use the **natural English** phrases.

> *example* **A** In situation 1, I think it's better to say something because maybe you can help.
> **B** I'm not sure. Perhaps the person is OK.

grammar *something, anything, nothing, etc.*

1 In the questionnaire, <u>underline</u> the words beginning *some* _____ , *any* _____ , and *no* _____ .

2 Answer with your partner.
1   Which three <u>underlined</u> words are about 'people'?
2   Circle the correct answer.
   a   With <u>someone</u>, <u>something</u>, <u>no one</u> and <u>nothing</u> use a positive / negative verb.
   b   Use <u>anything</u> and <u>anyone</u> in questions / positive sentences.
3   Rewrite these sentences.
   a   There's no one here. = _____ anyone here.
   b   I do nothing on Sundays. = _____ anything on Sundays.

3 Complete the table.

	PEOPLE		THINGS
positive	_____		something /ˈsʌmθɪŋ/
negative	_____ / not anyone /ˈeniwʌn/		_____ / _____
question	Is _____ there?		Do you want _____ ?

4 Complete the sentences with words from the table.

1 _____ told me about a new restaurant.
2 She doesn't know _____ in the other class.
3 There's _____ under the chair ... oh, it's my keys.
4 **A** Did you do _____ last night?
   B No, _____ .
5 I think there's _____ at the door.
6 It was very dark – I couldn't see _____ .
7 We phoned, but _____ answered.

5 **pronunciation** Practise the sentences.

go to **language reference** *and* **practice exercises** *p.140*

listen to this

tune in

1 What can you see in the pictures? Tell a partner.

2 (10.6) Listen to the first part of the conversation. Which picture is it about?

listen carefully

3 Listen to the whole conversation. Darren offers to do three things. What are they?

listening challenge

4 (10.7) Look at picture 2 and read the summary. Then listen and complete.

The man wants his [1] _____ from upstairs. His sister offers to [2] _____ . He asks her to put it on the [3] _____ . The sister offers to bring the [4] _____ too – the man says [5] _____ .

listen again with the **tapescript** *p.153*

---

5 (10.8) **natural English** pronunciation Listen and notice the pronunciation of *I'll* and *Shall I ...?* Practise the dialogues.

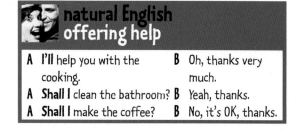

natural English
offering help

A I'll help you with the cooking.	**B** Oh, thanks very much.
A Shall I clean the bathroom?	**B** Yeah, thanks.
A Shall I make the coffee?	**B** No, it's OK, thanks.

6 Look at **tapescripts** 10.6 and 10.7 on *p.153*. Find examples of *I'll ...* and *Shall I ...?*

speaking it's your turn!

1 Work in A / B pairs.

A – go to *p.125*   B – go to *p.126*

writing

1 Read the first e-mail. Put the reply in the correct order.

> Hi, Zsuzsa
> I have a problem. My sister has to go to the hospital at 10.00. I can't go with her, because I have to go to a meeting in Budapest, but she doesn't want to go alone. Can you help?
> Best wishes, Feri

> ☐ Don't worry.
> ☐ Give me her phone number
> ☐ Best wishes, Zsuzsa
> 1 Hi, Feri
> ☐ I'll take your sister to the hospital.
> ☐ Have a good day in Budapest.
> ☐ and I can speak to her this evening.

2 Work in A / B pairs. Write an e-mail to your partner explaining a problem. Use the e-mail in **exercise 1** to help you. Send your e-mail, then reply to your partner's.

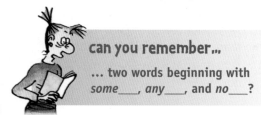

can you remember...

... two words beginning with *some___, any___,* and *no___*?

help with pronunciation and listening

---

pronunciation sounds and spelling /ʊ/, /uː/, /ʌ/, and /əʊ/

1 Put these words in the correct column in the table.

took	house	double	about
group	couple	could	soup
mouth	cousin	hour	foot
spoon	would	tooth	country

1 /aʊ/	2 /uː/	3 /ʌ/	4 /ʊ/
<u>out</u>	<u>soon</u>	<u>young</u>	<u>book</u>

2 **10.9** Listen to three words in each column. Which is missing?

3 Work with a partner.

A – quickly say three words from one column.

B – say the missing word.

---

listening connected speech

Important!
In spoken English, we link words / phrases together. (e.g. *Do you like* /djəˈlaɪk/). The pronunciation is sometimes different from the written form.

1 **10.10** Listen. Number the phrases in the order you hear them.

☐ shall I ...? /ʃəlaɪ/ ☐ would you ...? /ˈwʊdjə/

☐ I'll buy ... /aɪlbaɪ/ ☐ I can't do ... /aɪkɑːn(t)duː/

☐ could you ...? /ˈkʊdjə/ ☐ do you ...? /djʊ/

2 **10.11** Listen to this man's answerphone. What's his name? What's his wife's name?

3 **10.12** Listen to four messages. Match them with the pictures.

4 Listen to 10.12 again and complete.

1 _____ do my homework ...

  _____ all the countries in the EU?

  _____ ring me on my mobile?

2 _____ get the tickets for the cinema tonight?

3 _____ it for you.

4 _____ a table at the restaurant ...

  _____ Chinese or Thai?

Check with the tapescript on *p.153*. Practise the sentences.

ten review

grammar *something, anything, nothing, etc.*

1 Complete the questions with *anyone / anything*. Think about your answers.

---
my journey to class

1 Did you buy —— on the way to class?
2 Did you come to class with ——?
3 Did you have —— to eat on the journey?
4 Did you have —— to drink?
5 Did you talk to ——?
6 Did you read ——?
7 Did you listen to —— on the way?
8 Did you phone —— on your mobile?

---

2 Find a partner. Interview them using the questions, like this:

A Did you buy anything on the way to class today?

B Yes, I did. A magazine and some chocolate.

vocabulary *action verbs and parts of the body*

Work with a partner.   A – go to *p.126*.   B – go to *p.128*.

vocabulary *common phrases*

1 Order the words.

1 Joe / to / happened / what?
2 matter / the / what's?
3 need / you / do / help / any?
4 don't / very / look / well / you
5 bag / I / hand / give / can / you / a / that / with?

2 Match 1 to 5 in **exercise 1** with a to e below.

a There's something wrong with my computer.
b He broke his arm playing football.
c Thanks, that's very kind of you. It's very heavy.
d No, I feel terrible today.
e No, thanks, I'm fine.

natural English

1 Are the underlined phrases the same (S) or different (D)?

example   Thank you <u>very much</u>. / Thanks <u>a lot</u>. (S)

1 I got married <u>at 24</u>. / I got married <u>when I was 24.</u>
2 He can play the piano <u>very well</u>. / He can play the piano <u>quite well</u>.
3 <u>I can't cook very well</u>. / <u>I can't cook</u>.
4 A Shall I carry this for you?
   B <u>It's OK, thanks</u>. B <u>Yes, thanks</u>.

2 Check your answers using the **natural English** boxes in unit ten.

---

test yourself!

Now cover the REVIEW section and test yourself on unit ten.

test your vocabulary

From this unit:

1 complete four things babies can do at one year old: s _ _ _ e;
l _ _ _ h; w _ _ e goodbye;
p _ _ y with things
2 order the words:
I / a / lift / can / you / give?
with / there / wrong / something / is / car / my
that / kind / is / of / very / thanks / you
3 write five parts of the body that people have <u>two</u> of: *example* two arms (NOT ~~two noses~~)

score ☐ 12

gap-fill

Fill the gaps.

1 I can swim quite ——.
2 **A** —— I do the cleaning?
   B Oh, thank you.
3 It's dark; I can't see ——.
4 **A** Do you know —— in the other class?
   B No, no one.

score ☐ 4

error correction

Correct the errors.

1 I can to speak French.
2 Babies can walk when they have 10–12 months old.
3 I think is better to say nothing.
4 Don't worry. I help you.

score ☐ 4

total score ☐ 20

Look back at the unit contents on *p.79*. Tick ✓ the language you can use.

tick ✓ when you know this

natural English
- ☐ *How long does it take?*
- ☐ agreeing and disagreeing
- ☐ *get*
- ☐ recommending: *should* + verb

grammar
- ☐ comparative adjectives
- ☐ superlative adjectives

vocabulary
- ☐ shops and products
- ☐ adjectives (3)

reading
from A to B

lead-in

1 With a partner, match the opposites. You have two minutes!

~~old~~ easy practical common useless safe fast boring
difficult slow useful exciting impractical unusual dangerous ~~new~~

2 Which words describe a car? motorbike? computer? camera?

grammar comparative adjectives

1 Ask three people.

Have you got a bike /baɪk/ or a motorbike /ˈməʊtəbaɪk/?

If so, what kind is it, and when do you use it?

2 Look at the pictures. Complete the gaps with the size and price.

1 The bike (_____ cms) is **smaller than** the motorbike (_____ cms).

2 The motorbike (_____) is **more expensive than** the bike (_____).

3 **(11.1)** **pronunciation** Listen. Notice the pronunciation of
*small**er*** /ˈsmɔːlə/ *th**a**n* /ðən/. Then listen and practise.

4 Work in A pairs and B pairs. As – answer the questions on *p.122.*
Bs – answer the questions on *p.128.*

5 Work in A / B pairs. A – close your book. B – ask A your questions.

example   B   Which is bigger – the bike or the motorbike?

A   The motorbike's bigger.

Then change roles.

Price	€389
Size	102cms

Price	€10,499
Size	117cms

6 Complete the table.

short adjectives (one syllable) or adjectives ending in –y e.g. *happy /happier*		long adjectives	
adjective	**comparative**	**adjective**	**comparative**
cheap	cheap _er_ (+ than)	difficult	_more difficult_ (+ than)
big	big ___	useful	_____
fast	fast ___	practical	_____
safe	safe ___	common	_____
easy	eas ___ NOT ~~easyer~~	dangerous	_____
slow	slow ___	comfortable	_____

irregular adjectives (two syllables or more)	
adjective	**comparative**
good	_____ (+ than)
bad	_____

7 Complete with a comparative adjective. Make some sentences true and some false.

example Planes are *slower* than buses. (false)

1 Cars are _____ than buses.

2 Planes are _____ than trains.

3 Going by bike is _____ than walking.

4 Taxis are _____ than trains.

5 Walking is _____ than driving.

6 Buses are _____ than planes.

Read your sentences to a partner. He / She has to say if they are true or false.

go to **language reference** *and* **practice exercises** *p.141*

read on

1 Read the first paragraph of the article. Circle the correct answer.

In the article, the journalists try some unusual forms of transport to find the best / cheapest way.

2 Read the article. Circle the correct answer.

1 The sedan chair was cheaper / more expensive than the scooter.

2 Rollerblading was slower / faster than the sedan chair.

3 The scooter was faster / slower than the rollerblades.

4 Rollerblading was / wasn't easy.

5 Alex did / didn't do all the journey in the sedan chair.

6 Pete felt / didn't feel very safe on the scooter.

Quicker than a car?

City traffic is awful – so we decided to try some different ways of getting around. Our test journey was between two famous art galleries – Tate Modern and Tate Britain. By taxi it takes 10–20 minutes, and costs about £6. This is what happened to our journalists …

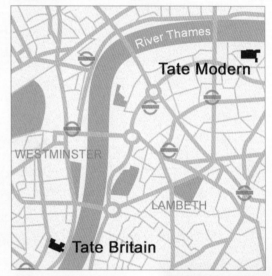

River Thames

Tate Modern

WESTMINSTER

LAMBETH

Tate Britain

ROLLERBLADES

● Fantastic – and you can do some sightseeing in London at the same time! It was also good for the environment and very **healthy**.

● I'm new to rollerblading, and it was very difficult to stop without a tree or a wall. It was quite uncomfortable and I got very **tired**.

cost £60 for the rollerblades

time 35 minutes

healthy (adj) /ˈhelθi/ a **healthy** activity is good for your body

tired (adj) /ˈtaɪəd/ if you are **tired**, you want to sleep

battery (n) /ˈbætri/

glossary

SAMSON

SEDAN CHAIR

Alex Hanford

- I felt like Cleopatra! The chair looked great, and everybody was looking at me. It was a hot day, but it was cool and comfortable.

- Very, very slow! The four people carrying me only took me 200 metres.

cost £275 for the chair, plus £160 for the four porters

time 18 minutes for 200 metres – and another hour to walk the rest of the way

ELECTRIC SCOOTER

Pete Clark

- Very nice! Easy to start and drive, and faster than driving a car or walking.

- It felt a bit dangerous, and the **battery** needs recharging after 15 kms.

cost £550 for the scooter

time 12 minutes

---

3 **natural English** (11.2) Listen. Match 1 to 3 with a to c. Practise the dialogues with a partner.

> **natural English**
> ## How long does it take?
>
> 1 **How long does it take** to walk to the station?
> 2 **How long does it take** to get to work?
> 3 **How long does it take** by scooter?
> a **It takes about** half an hour.
> b **Not long.**
> c **It takes a long time.**

4 **Think!** How long does it take to get from your home to:

the station?   school?

the post office?   *your ideas*

Ask a partner. Use language in the **natural English** box.

---

speaking it's your turn!

1 **Think!** Read the sentences. What do you think? Why?

Do you agree?	yes	no	don't know
Bikes are safer than motorbikes.			
Computers are more useful than TVs.			
Modern houses are better to live in than old houses.			
Women's clothes are more expensive than men's clothes.			
Saturdays are better than Sundays.			
Your sentence:			

2 **natural English** (11.3) Read the box and listen. Which answers do <u>you</u> agree with?

>
> **natural English**
> ## agreeing and disagreeing
>
> 'Bikes are safer than motorbikes.'
> **I agree** (with that). NOT ~~I'm agree~~
> **It depends.** (= yes and no)
>
> 'Computers are more useful than TVs.'
> **Yes, that's true.**
> **I'm not so sure.**

3 Talk to different people. Say a sentence from **exercise 1**. Do they agree? Why / Why not?

Saturdays are better than Sundays.

It depends, because ...

can you remember ...

... the comparative forms of these words?
cheap *cheaper*
common   fast   comfortable   big
good   interesting   easy   happy

wordbooster

shops and products

1 Work alone. Write one more thing you can buy in each place. Use the pictures to help you, or write your own ideas.

shops	products
butcher's	chicken and _____
furniture shop	tables and _____
baker's	bread and _____
shoe shop	shoes and _____
record shop	cassettes and _____
chemist	aspirin and _____
clothes shop	shirts and _____
supermarket	sugar and _____
department store	clothes and _____
post office	envelopes and _____

2 pronunciation Listen. <u>Underline</u> the main stress in the words in exercise 1. Practise saying the words.

3 natural English Read the natural English box. What does *get* mean here?

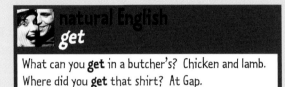

> **natural English**
> **get**
>
> What can you **get** in a butcher's? Chicken and lamb.
> Where did you **get** that shirt? At Gap.

4 Ask your partner about the shops / products in exercise 1.

example   A What can you get in a shoe shop?
            B Shoes and ...

5 Ask people where they got their clothes / personal objects.

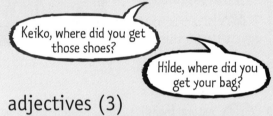

Keiko, where did you get those shoes?

Hilde, where did you get your bag?

adjectives (3)

1 Check any new adjectives in a dictionary. With a partner, write an example for each thing.

1 a **popular** sport (e.g. football) _____
2 a **healthy** /ˈhelθi/ drink _____
3 a **lucky** /ˈlʌki/ number _____
4 a **modern** building _____
5 a **busy** /ˈbɪzi/ place _____
6 a **common** /ˈkɒmən/ name _____
7 a **wonderful** /ˈwʌndəfl/ actor _____
8 a **rich** country _____
9 a **poor** /pɔː/ country _____

2 Listen. Are your answers the same?

3 Find a new partner. Say your answers in a different order. Your partner has to say what it is.

example   A The station.
            B A busy place?
            A That's right.

listening
how to ... recommend

can you remember ...

... the names of eight shops? Tell a partner.

lead-in

1   Can you **recommend** two things from this list? Tell a partner.

   a record shop   a shoe shop   a book shop
   a department store   a hairdresser   a nightclub
   example   I really like Discopiú. I get all my CDs there.

2   (11.6) **natural English**   Listen and complete.

>
> ## natural English
> ### recommending: *should* + verb
>
> 👍 **You should** go and see that new Johnny Depp film – _____ .
> 👍 **You should** visit the Tate Modern – _____ .
> 👎 **Don't** go to that new French restaurant – _____ .
>
>

3   **pronunciation** Listen again. What's the pronunciation of *should*? Practise the sentences.

4   In the table write six things you recommend or don't recommend.

	☺	☹
example a film	*Lost in Translation*	*Titanic*
a film		
a bar / restaurant		
a museum		
a book		
a TV programme		
a place to go on holiday		

5   Work in small groups. Use the **natural English** phrases to recommend the things in your table. Give reasons.

go to **language reference** *and* **practice exercises** *p.142*

listen to this

tune in

1   (11.7) Listen to the beginning of a radio programme.

   1   What's the name of the programme?
   2   What does the presenter ask people to recommend?

listen carefully

2   Listen. Which three places do the people talk about?

3   Listen again. Circle the correct answers.

   speaker 1 says you should:
   1   go in summer / in winter
   2   get around by bus / by water bus
   3   go to the Cannaregio area for restaurants / museums

   speaker 2 says:
   1   you should go in late spring / in July and August
   2   the best way to see the place is by bus / by car

   speaker 3 says you should:
   1   see the city by taxi / by boat
   2   go swimming in the river / go shopping

listening challenge

4   (11.8) Listen. Which holiday does Ben like best?

listen again with the **tapescript** *p.154*

5   Do you know any of these places? If so, what do you think of them? Which <u>new</u> place would you like to go to?

grammar superlative adjectives

1 Can you remember how to complete these sentences? Use the adjectives to help you. Then check with tapescript 11.7.

   friendly   romantic

  1 Venice is probably the _____ _____ city in the world.
  2 Cairo has the _____ people I know.

2 With a partner, complete the table.

ADJECTIVE	COMPARATIVE	SUPERLATIVE
happy	happier	the _____
beautiful	more beautiful	the _____
interesting	_____	_____
hot	_____	_____
expensive	_____	_____
good	_____	_____
bad	_____	_____

3 Circle the correct answer.

Use comparative adjectives (e.g. *bigger, more comfortable*) to compare one thing with one other thing / other things in a group.

Use superlative adjectives (e.g. *the biggest, the most comfortable*) to compare one thing with one other thing / other things in a group.

4 **(11.9)** **pronunciation** Listen. Do you hear the underlined 't'?

  1 It's the mos<u>t</u> beautiful place I know.
  2 He's the oldes<u>t</u> man in the class.
  3 She's the bes<u>t</u> student.
  4 That's the mos<u>t</u> expensive chair.
  5 It's the wors<u>t</u> place to eat in town.

Practise the sentences.

go to **language reference** *and* **practice exercises** *p.141–142*

5 With a partner, write six sentences about the people in the pictures. Compare with a new partner.

  example Number 2 is the oldest.

speaking it's your turn!

1 **Think!** What should tourists do in your country? Where should they go?

  the most famous / interesting places
  the most beautiful beaches
  things to buy
  ways to get around (e.g. car or train)

They should go to ...

They should buy ...

2 Tell a partner about the things / places you recommend, and why.

writing

Correct ten more spelling mistakes.

  ... and then we spent a few days in Switzerland.
     really
  It's a realy beautifull place and we were lucky with the wether. Zurich was interesting and was the bigest town we stayed in. From ther we took the train and stoped in Lucerne. Then we traveled on down to the Italien part. We stayed in Lugano for two days to visit my oldest freind, Caroline. She's English but she is married to a Swisse docter.

can you remember ...

... the superlative forms?
expensive old good bad
beautiful comfortable small

extended speaking

town survey

 ## collect ideas

1   Do you like your town / city?
Why / Why not? Tell a partner.

 ## prepare a survey

2   In groups of three, write six more superlative questions in the table. Use these places.

> street   restaurant   department store
> school   park / square   tourist attraction
> shop (clothes shop, etc.)   *your own ideas*

3   Write <u>your</u> answers in the 'me' column.

 ## listen

4   **11.10** Listen to Patience interviewing Roger and Lorelei about New York. What questions does she ask them?

5   Listen again. Do Roger and Lorelei agree?

 ## do the survey

6   Interview the two students in your group. Write their answers in the table

7   Interview a partner from another group. Write their answers under 'student 4'.

 ## compare answers

8   With your partner, look at all the survey answers. Which are the best things in your town? Tell the class.

Opinion survey – our town

	me	student 2	student 3	student 4
What's the most interesting area?				
What's the best café?				
What's the ugliest building?				
_____ ?				
_____ ?				
_____ ?				
_____ ?				
_____ ?				
_____ ?				

eleven review

grammar comparative adjectives

Write the opposites. Compare with a partner.

example   faster *slower*

~~faster~~	more expensive	safer	more difficult	worse
more boring	younger	quieter	smaller	colder

grammar superlative adjectives

1   With a partner, write a sentence about each picture with the correct superlative adjective.

example   Picture 1 is the longest river in the world (the Nile in Egypt).

2   Read your sentences to another pair. Do they agree?

3   Listen. Answer the questions.

1   Were you right about each picture?

2   What important fact do you learn about each picture?

vocabulary adjectives (3)

go to **pairwork** *p.129*

natural English

1   ~~Cross out~~ the incorrect word in each sentence.

example   My daughter left school at eighteen ~~years~~.

1   How long time does it take?
2   I am agree with you.
3   It's depends.
4   You should to go and see him.
5   Where did you get buy that watch?
6   Don't to go there – it's dangerous.

2   Check your answers using the **natural English** boxes in unit eleven.

friends   twelve

tick ✓ when you know this

natural English
- [ ] *How about you?*
- [ ] *mostly*
- [ ] phoning a friend
- [ ] telephone introductions
- [ ] showing you (don't)
      understand

grammar
- [ ] present continuous
- [ ] present simple vs continuous

vocabulary
- [ ] clothes
- [ ] telephoning

reading
who are they?

lead-in

1 **Think!** Think about the friends you usually go out with.

How many are there in your group?

Are they all men, all women, or both?

Are they all the same age?

Where do you go together, and what do you do?

When / How often do you see them?

2 [12.1] Listen to Roger. What are his answers?

3 [12.2] **natural English** Look at the box and listen. What's the pronunciation of *How about you*?

> **natural English**
> ### *How about you?*
>
> **A** Have you got a group of friends you go out with?
> **B** Yes – my old school friends. **How about you?** (= And you?)
> **A** Yes, friends from work.

4 Practise the dialogue.

5 Get up and ask people the questions in **exercise 1**.

The luncheon of the boating party

Pierre Auguste Renoir, one of the most important Impressionist painters, painted *The Luncheon of the Boating Party* during the summer of 1881.

The Restaurant Fournaise, which you can see in the picture,
5 is in Chatou, to the west of Paris, on the River Seine. In the 1880s, Parisians started to have more time to **enjoy** themselves. If they wanted to get out of the dirty, noisy capital at the weekends, the new **railway** could take them to places along the river where they could **relax**, eat, **sail**, swim,
10 and dance.

The people in this painting were all Renoir's friends. The young woman on the left with the dog was Renoir's girlfriend, <u>Aline Charigot</u>. They got married a year after Renoir finished the painting, and they had a very happy life
15 together. Behind her is <u>Alphonse Fournaise</u>, the son of the **owner** of the restaurant, and the woman standing near him is his sister, <u>Alphonsine</u>. Opposite Aline, wearing a hat and sitting on a chair, is <u>Gustave Caillebotte</u>, an artist and close friend of Renoir. Also in the group with Caillebotte is the
20 actress, <u>Angèle</u>, and the Italian journalist, <u>Maggiolo</u>. Two more actresses are in the painting: one in the centre, drinking from a glass, and the other on the right. The man in the black top hat, <u>Charles Ephrussi</u>, was a rich banker and art collector, and the man he is talking to in the brown jacket
25 was probably the poet <u>Jules Laforgue</u>.

Today it is in the Phillips Collection in Washington D.C., and many people think it is one of the greatest paintings in the world.

read on

1 **Cover the text. With a partner, answer the questions about the painting. Guess if you don't know.**

1 Who painted the picture?
  a Van Gogh   b Picasso   c Renoir
2 When did he paint it?
  a 1841   b 1881   c 1921
3 Which country is it in?
  a France   b Spain   c Holland
4 Where is it?
  a a restaurant   b a hotel   c a house

2 **Read the first two paragraphs. Find the answers to exercise 1.**

3 **Read the rest of the text. Who were the people, 1–8?**

example   1 Alphonse Fournaise: son of restaurant owner

4 **Do you like the painting? Tell a partner why.**

grammar present continuous

1 Look at the picture. True or false?

1 One of the actresses **is drinking** from a glass.
2 All the women **are wearing** hats.
3 The girl on the balcony **isn't smiling**.
4 Someone **is eating** a piece of bread.
5 The woman on the left **is playing** with a dog.
6 Alphonse and Alphonsine **aren't sitting down**.

2 Complete the table.

PRESENT CONTINUOUS: *BE + -ING*

Use the present continuous to say what is happening <u>now</u> or <u>at the moment</u>.

positive		negative	
I' ___		I' ___ not	
He / She' ___	working	He / She ___	working
You / We / They' ___		You / We / They ___	

questions		short answers	
___ you / we / they	working?	Yes, we / they ___ .	
___ he / she		No, he / she ___ .	

spelling						
go *going*	say _____	swim _____	smoke _____
work _____	play _____	sit _____	smile _____
talk _____	study _____	get _____	live _____

3 Look at the picture on *p.96* and complete the sentences. Use these verbs in the present continuous form.

drink   stand   eat   smoke   look   wear   sit   sail

1 Some people _____ on the river.
2 No one _____ coffee.
3 Caillebotte _____ a jacket.
4 The actress next to Caillebotte _____ at him.
5 Alphonse _____ next to Renoir's girlfriend.
6 Caillebotte _____ opposite the woman with the dog.
7 The men _____ anything.
8 Caillebotte _____ a cigarette.

Read your sentences to a partner. Are they the same?

4 Listen to the party. Then, with a partner, write sentences using the present continuous.

Someone …   *People …*

go to **language reference** *and* **practice exercises** *p.142–143*

5 Write six questions about your class at the moment.

examples   **Is anyone wearing** a blue jacket?
Is Bettina standing or sitting?

What are Mia and Dan doing?
Who's working with Xavier?

6 Find a partner. Ask and answer your questions.

speaking it's your turn!

1 **Think!** Look at the painting below. Think of six things to say about it.

It's near a river.

A woman's holding a black umbrella.

2 Work in small groups. Say your sentences. You get one point for each sentence which is different from the others. Who has the most points?

can you remember …

… six things people are doing in the Renoir painting? Shut your book and write them down.

wordbooster

clothes

1 What's each person wearing? Tell a partner, using words from the box.

shoes	skirt /skɜːt/	shirt /ʃɜːt/	tie /taɪ/	boots	jumper /'dʒʌmpə/
jeans	top	trainers	jacket	T-shirt /'tiːʃɜːt/	
coat /kəʊt/	suit /suːt/	dress	hat	trousers /'traʊzəz/	

2 Cover the words and say what each person is wearing.

3 Sit back to back with a partner. Can you remember what your partner is wearing? Tell him/her. Then do the same with a new partner.

telephoning

1 Read the text. How many times did Terry phone his lawyer?

Terry tried to ring his lawyer, Mr Donald, this morning.

The first time he called, the line was engaged, so he rang again ten minutes later.

This time he got the answerphone and left a message – *My name is Terry Brown and my number is 248 9936. Could you ring me as soon as possible, please?*

He waited for an hour but his lawyer didn't ring back, so he phoned again.

Mr Donald was busy, but Terry spoke to his secretary and left another message.

Nothing happened. He rang again at 12.30 but there was no answer. Mr Donald was out – buying a mobile phone!

2 Answer the questions.

1 What happened the first time he phoned?
2 What happened the second time?
3 What happened the third time?

3 Underline all the verbs that mean *to telephone*.

4 Go to *p.126* and complete the text.

5 **Listen and check. Practise reading the text aloud with a partner.**

listening
how to ... use the phone

can you remember ...

... eight words or phrases about phoning?

lead-in

1 Think! Think about your answers.

Have you got a mobile phone?

☐ If yes ...	☐ If no ...
What kind is it?	Do you want one?
Do you play games on it?	Why / Why not?
Do you send photos / texts on it?	When do you use your normal phone mostly?
Where do you use it mostly?	How often do you use it?
Do you use it mostly to ring friends, family, or for work?	Who do you ring mostly?

2 **natural English** Listen. Do you hear the 't' in *mostly*? Practise the dialogues.

 **natural English**
mostly

mostly = most of the time / in most situations

A Have you got a mobile?
B Yes, I use it **mostly** for work.
C When do you use your mobile?
D **Mostly** in the evenings and at weekends.

3 Work in small groups. Talk about your answers to **exercise 1.**

grammar present simple vs continuous

1 Complete the sentences about Emma. What tense is used?

Emma Waters

27, single, fashion designer at Johnson Fabrics, lives with her best friend (Kate)

1 Emma _____ on a sofa.
2 She _____ jeans.
3 She _____ her boyfriend.
4 She _____ a bar of chocolate.

2 Look at the questions in **lead-in exercise 1.** What tense is used?

3 Match the sentence endings.

1 My parents <u>have</u> lunch   a at the moment.
2 My parents <u>are having</u> lunch   b one of my shirts today.
3 My brother <u>wears</u>   c jeans a lot.
4 My brother<u>'s wearing</u>   d at one o'clock every day.

4 Circle the correct answers.

Use the present simple / present continuous for things that happen *every day / week, a lot, often*, etc.

Use the present simple / present continuous for things happening *at the moment, now, today*, etc.

5 Fill the gaps with a verb in the present simple or continuous.

1 A Where's Bruno?
   B In the study. He _____ a book.
2 I usually _____ about seven hours a night.
3 A _____ Claudia _____ her homework at the moment?
   B No, she _____ TV.
4 A What time _____ you normally _____ work?
   B Eight o'clock in the morning.
5 Gary usually _____ jeans and a T-shirt, but he's got a job interview today, so he _____ a suit.

go to **language reference** *and* **practice exercises** *p.143*

listen to this

tune in

1 Listen to Emma on the phone. Does she know Tom?

Tom
Trisha

2 **natural English** Complete the dialogue. Then listen again to check your answers.

Practise with a partner.

natural English
phoning a friend

A Hello?
B Is _____ Tom? (NOT ~~Are you Tom?~~)
A Yeah, _____ .
B Oh, hi Tom. _____ Emma. (NOT ~~I am Emma~~)

listen carefully

3 Listen to the whole conversation. Write T (true) or F (false).

1 Trisha's out at the moment.
2 She went to buy clothes for a party.
3 She'll be back before lunch.
4 Emma leaves a message.
5 She wants to speak to Trisha after 3.00.
6 Emma's phone number is 642 1689.

4 Listen again. Complete the message for Trisha.

Trisha, can ...

listening challenge

5 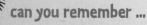 Trisha rings Emma at work. Listen and answer.

1 What did Trisha buy this morning?
2 Why does Emma want to speak to her?
3 What number does Trisha give Emma?

listen again with the **tapescript** *p.155*

6 natural English Read the box. Then listen and tick ✓ the phrases you hear.

Practise both dialogues with a partner.

natural English
telephone introductions

Can I speak to Emma Waters, **please?**	**Could I speak to** Emma Waters, **please?**
Yes, **who's calling, please?**	Yes, **who's speaking, please?**
It's Trisha Morgan.	**My name's** Trisha Morgan.

writing

1 With a partner, complete the conversation.

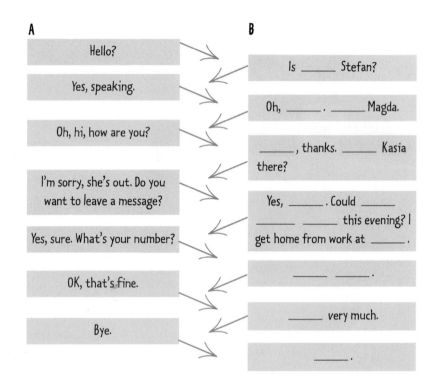

A

Hello?

Yes, speaking.

Oh, hi, how are you?

I'm sorry, she's out. Do you want to leave a message?

Yes, sure. What's your number?

OK, that's fine.

Bye.

B

Is _____ Stefan?

Oh, _____ . _____ Magda.

_____ , thanks. _____ Kasia there?

Yes, _____ . Could _____ _____ _____ this evening? I get home from work at _____ .

_____ _____ .

_____ very much.

_____ .

2 Practise the conversation with your partner.

3 With your partner, write the message Stefan leaves for Kasia.

speaking it's your turn!

1 Work in A / B pairs. A – go to *p.129*. B – go to *p.126*.

2 Change roles. Complete your new role card and do the role play.

can you remember ...
... two ways of asking for another person on the phone, and two ways of introducing yourself?

help with pronunciation and listening

---

pronunciation consonant groups

1 (12.9) **Many words have two consonant sounds at the beginning. Listen and practise.**

skirt   trainers
spell   clothes   dress
problem   stand

Be careful! Don't say /eskɜːt/ **or** /sekɜːt/.

2 With a partner, complete the words.
1 **Sp**eak **Sp**anish in **Sp**ain and South America.
2 Don't **dr**ink and **dr**_____ .
3 **Tr**avel by public **tr**_____ .
4 Eat **br**own **br**ead for **br**_____ .
5 **Pr**_____ your **pr**onunciation every day.
6 Don't wear a **sk**_____ for **sk**iing.
7 **St**_____ sleeping and **st**art **st**udying.
8 Wear **tr**_____ when you're **tr**avelling.

3 (12.10) **Listen and check. Practise the sentences.**

---

listening being an active listener

Important!
When you're listening, it's important to show you understand, or <u>don't</u> understand.

1 (12.11) **Jean-Louis is on holiday in Britain. Look at the photo and listen to conversation 1. Does he understand everything?**

2 Listen again and complete.

J-L	Excuse me.
Man	Yes?
J-L	I'm looking for the bus stop for the number three.
Man	Ah, right, OK, you see the department store?
J-L	_____ ?
Man	That big shop there, on the corner.
J-L	_____ , _____ .
Man	OK, turn left there, and that's where the bus stop is.
J-L	_____ _____ – thank you very much.

3 Listen to conversation 2 in a café. Does he understand:
1 the first question?
2 the second question?
3 the third question?

4 Listen to conversation 3 in a tourist information office.
1 What does he want to know?
2 Does he understand the first answer?
3 Does he understand the second answer?

5 natural English Complete the box with words / phrases from tapescript 12.11.

> **natural English**
> **showing you (don't) understand**
>
> (Ah, right,) OK.   Sorry? (What's that?)
> _____   _____ ?
> _____   Could _____ ?
> _____

---

twelve review

vocabulary clothes

go to **pairwork** *p.129.*

grammar present continuous and present simple

1 Work with a partner. Take turns to mime the phrases. Your partner has to tell you what you're doing.

> have a drink   do the housework
> wash your hair   clean your teeth
> do nothing   play cards
> write a letter   ~~read the paper~~
> use your mobile   drive to school

test your partner
– *You're reading the paper.*

– *That's right.*

2 Complete the sentences using phrases from **exercise 1**.

examples I <u>sometimes wash my hair</u> before breakfast. (sometimes)
            He <u>doesn't play cards</u> in the evenings.(not)

1 I _____ after breakfast. (always)
2 He _____ in the evenings. (not)
3 I _____ in the car. (never)
4 She _____ at lunchtime. (not)
5 They _____ at the weekends.(often)
6 He _____ every week. (not)
7 I _____ when I get home in the evening. (sometimes)
8 She _____ in the morning. (not)

3 Read your sentences to a partner. Are they the same?

natural English

1 Put the <u>underlined</u> phrases in order. Use contractions (e.g. *it's*).

1 I've got a laptop. <u>use / I / mostly / work / for / it</u>.
2 A I've got two brothers and a sister. <u>you / about / how</u>?
  B Oh, I've only got one sister.
3 A Hello?
  B <u>Jack / is / hi / oh / that</u>?
  A Yeah, speaking.
  B <u>is / it / hi / Carole / oh</u>.
4 A <u>please / Robin Lowe / speak / I / can / to</u>?
  B <u>calling / yes / is / who / please</u>?
  A <u>name / Rachel Morales / is / my</u>.

2 Check your answers using the **natural English** boxes in unit twelve.

---

test yourself!

test your vocabulary

From this unit, write down:

1 seven more items of clothing:
   shoes, trousers, ...
2 a word to complete these sentences about telephoning:
   I rang but there was no _____.
   What's your phone _____ ?
   I got her answer_____.
   She left a _____.
   Ring me as soon as _____.
3 the present continuous form of these verbs:
   example sit / I'm sitting
   live, swim, study, get, smile

score 17

gap-fill

Fill the gaps.

1 A When do you go to the gym?
  B _____ at weekends.
2 A I see my parents every week.
    How _____ you?
  B Not very often.
3 A Did you ring him?
  B Yes, but the line was _____ .
4 A Did you phone her?
  B Yes, I rang her on my _____ .

score 4

error correction

Correct the errors.

1 He has lunch at the moment.
2 She doesn't wearing a hat today.
3 On the phone:
  A Hello?
  B Hi. Are you Pamela?
4 A Who's calling, please?
  B I am Mark Andrews.

score 4

total score 25

Look back at the unit contents on *p.95*. Tick ✓ the language you can use.

plans

thirteen

tick ✓ when you know this

natural English
- [ ] *What are you doing tonight?*
- [ ] *Do you ever ...?*
- [ ] inviting and responding
- [ ] making plans together

grammar
- [ ] *be going to* + verb
- [ ] *might* + verb

vocabulary
- [ ] verb + preposition
- [ ] kinds of film

reading
a new life

lead-in

Think! Why do people go and live abroad? Do any of your friends / family live abroad now? If so, where and why? Tell a partner.

read on

1 Read about Melissa and Scott. Why do people want to go on their TV programme? Do you have programmes like this in your country?

LIFESTYLE **Get a new life**

Melissa Porter and Scott Huggins present a TV programme which makes it possible for one family to follow their

dream of living abroad. The family only have a short period of time to prepare, then Melissa and Scott help them to find a home and look for jobs (and sometimes schools) in the new country – but only for the first month. At the the end of that time, the family have a choice: do they want to stay and live in their new country without help, or accept free air tickets and return to Britain?

glossary **dream** (n) /driːm/ something good you want to happen in your life

Meet Mike and Eva Prosser. They want to go and live in Krakow, Poland. Eva's grandparents are Polish and Eva would like her two sons, Matthew (7) and Tomas (4), to spend time in Poland and learn the language. Her husband, Mike, is a builder and he **hopes** to **get a job** in Krakow now that Poland is in the European Union. He doesn't speak Polish but he is going to take lessons when they arrive. Eva speaks Polish quite well, so she might find a job more easily than Mike. She's going to phone some companies in Krakow when they get there.

At the moment they're selling their house in England, and with the money they want to buy a bigger place in Poland, where houses are cheaper. For the first month, they are planning to rent a flat near the grandparents, but they might have to buy some furniture.

They're going to send Matthew to **primary school** in Krakow. They're not sure what they're going to do with Tomas, but they might send him to **nursery school**.

2 Read about Mike and Eva. Answer true or false.

1 Eva wants her sons to speak Polish.
2 Mike hopes to find work because his wife is Polish.
3 They plan to buy a house when they arrive.
4 Houses are cheaper in Poland.
5 They are going to stay with Eva's grandparents.

3 Read the article again then think about the questions below. Talk in small groups.

1 Is it a good idea to sell the house before they go to Poland?
2 Is it better to rent a flat, or stay in a hotel when they arrive?
3 Should they learn Polish before they go, or after they arrive?
4 Should their children go to a local school when they arrive?
5 Is it a good idea for both parents to look for work?
6 Is it better to go to a city (like Krakow) or a smaller town?

grammar *be going to* + verb; *might* /maɪt/ + verb

1 Look at these sentences from the article. Do they refer to the present or the future?

Mike **is going to** take lessons when they arrive.

She's going to phone some companies when they get there.

They're going to send Matthew to primary school in Krakow.

2 Complete the table.

BE GOING TO				
positive			**negative**	
I' ___ He / She' ___ You / We / They' ___		going to do it.	I' ___ He / She ___ We / You / They ___	going to do it.
questions			**short answers**	
___ you / they ___ he / she		going to do it?	Yes, I ___ . No, he ___ . Yes, they ___ .	

3 Cover the table and complete the dialogues.

1 A _____ he going _____ learn the language?
  B Yes, he is.
2 A _____ you _____ to live there for a long time?
  B No, I don't think so.
3 A I _____ not going _____ get a job.
  B Oh, right.
4 A Are they _____ to buy a house when they arrive?
  B No, they _____ .

4 **pronunciation** Listen and check. How does the speaker pronounce *going to* in questions 2 and 4? Practise the dialogues with a partner. You can say /ˈgəʊɪŋ tə/ or /ˈgənə/.

5 Look at the article again. Write <u>yes</u>, <u>no</u> or <u>not sure</u>.

1 Is Matthew going to start school in Poland?

2 Is Tomas going to go to nursery school in Poland?

3 Are they going to buy any furniture?

4 Is Eva going to phone any companies in Krakow?

6 <u>Underline</u> the correct answers.

1 You use *be going to* + **verb** to talk about the present / future.

2 You use it to talk about a plan which you think is sure / possible.

3 You use *might* (*not*) + **verb** to talk about something which is sure / possible.

7 <u>Underline</u> the correct answer.

1 In the first month, the family might / is going to rent a flat.

2 Melissa and Scott might / are going to help the family.

3 Mike might / is going to get a job.

4 Mike might / is going to study Polish when he arrives.

5 After the first month, the family might / is going to stay in Poland.

8 (13.2) **natural English** Listen and complete the answers.

---

natural English
What are you doing tonight?

To ask about plans, you can say, 'What are you going to do tonight?' But it is more natural in spoken English to ask, 'What are you doing tonight?'

What are you doing tonight?	I'm _____.
What are you doing tomorrow?	I _____.
What are you doing this weekend?	_____ much.

---

9 Write the correct date for:

tonight   next week

tomorrow   next weekend

this Saturday

10 With a partner, talk about your plans. Use the words in **exercise 9.**

example **A** What are you doing tonight?

B I'm going to study. And you?

A I don't know. I might go and see a friend.

go to **language reference** *and* **practice exercises** *p.144*

writing

Think! You are going to 'get a new life' abroad. Complete the form with your plans.

LIFESTYLE Get a new life

PERSONAL INFORMATION

name _____

address _____

telephone number _____

e-mail address _____

marital status _____

job _____

YOUR PLANS

Which country / city do you want to live in?

_____

Why? _____

Where are you going to stay when you get there?

☐ student accommodation   ☐ hotel

☐ rent a flat   ☐ with friends / family

☐ other _____

What are you going to do?

☐ work (if so, what?) _____   ☐ study (if so, what?)
_____

☐ other _____

Are you going to learn the language? _____

If so, how? _____

Other plans: _____

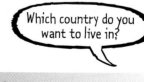

speaking it's your turn!

Work in small groups. Talk about your plans. Which plan is best?

Which country do you want to live in?

can you remember ...

... three definite plans, and three possible plans for the Prosser family? Tell a partner.

wordbooster

verb + preposition

1 Complete the sentences with verbs from the box. Then compare with a partner.

look	wait	listen	agree
spend	speak	think	pay

1 How much do you _____ **for** a newspaper?
2 Do you often _____ **to** the radio in the car?
3 Do you usually _____ **with** your friends' ideas?
4 Do you ever _____ **to** your friends in English?
5 Do you ever _____ a lot of money **on** perfume?
6 Do you ever _____ **after** other people's children?
7 Do you often have to _____ **for** buses and trains?
8 Do you often _____ **about** your future?

2 (13.3) **natural English** Listen. Match the questions and answers.

natural English
Do you ever ...?

Ever means *at any time*. It is very common in questions.

1 **Do you ever** speak to your family in English?
2 **Do you ever** eat Chinese food?
3 **Do you ever** come to school by bike?
a Er, sometimes.
b No, never.
c Yes, often.

3 Practise the natural English questions with a partner. Give true answers.

4 With a new partner, ask and answer the questions in **exercise 1**.

kinds of film

1 Match the words and pictures.

cartoon /kɑːˈtuːn/	comedy /ˈkɒmədi/	horror film /ˈhɒrə fɪlm/
thriller /ˈθrɪlə/	war film /ˈwɔː fɪlm/	romantic comedy
musical	action film	

2 Think! What kinds of film do you enjoy? Think of the names of some films.

example I enjoy comedies – like *Meet the Family* or *Austin Powers*.

Tell a partner.

listening
how to... invite someone

lead-in

1 Think! Think about these questions.

What was the last film you saw?

When did you see it?

Did you like it? Why / Why not?

Ask three people. Did you see the same films?

2 Look at the advert. Then complete the questions below with words from the box.

Apollo Cinema

Bridget Jones – The Edge of Reason (15)

Romantic comedy starring Renée Zellweger and Hugh Grant

Bridget Jones is happy with her boyfriend, but when her ex-boss (Hugh Grant) comes back into her life, things start to get interesting ...

108 minutes   Showing at: 4.10 6.20 8.30

who   how   what (x3)   where   when

1	**What**'s on at the cinema tonight?	*Bridget Jones – The Edge of Reason.*
2	_____ kind of film is it?	It's a romantic comedy.
3	_____'s it about?	It's about a woman and her boyfriend, and her ex-manager who has romantic ideas about her.
4	_____'s in it?	Renée Zellweger and Hugh Grant.
5	_____'s it on?	The Apollo Cinema.
6	_____ does it start?	4.10, 6.20, or 8.30.
7	_____ long is it?	108 minutes.

3 (13.4) Listen and check.

4 Work in A / B pairs. A – go to *p.127*. B – go to *p.128*. Find the answers to the questions in **exercise 2**.

5 Ask your partner about their film using the questions in **exercise 2**. Which film do you prefer?

inviting

1 (13.5) **natural English** Listen. Tick ✓ the phrases you hear.

natural English
inviting and responding

Would you like to ...? is a little more formal than *Do you want to ...?*

Would you like to go out tonight?
Do you want to go for a drink?
Would you like to go to the cinema tonight?

Yes, great. / Yeah, OK.
Sorry, I'm a bit busy.
Sorry, I can't tonight. Maybe tomorrow?

2 pronunciation Listen again and practise. Stress the underlined syllables.

3 Practise inviting and answering with a partner. Use the pictures and your ideas.

listen to this

tune in

1 Listen to the beginning of the conversation. Are they friends, or is this a business call?

2 Listen again. Complete the sentences.

Hello, _____ Toby?   Who's _____?

_____ Gina.   _____ this evening?

listen carefully

3 Listen to the whole conversation and complete the notes.

films on:
1 *Collateral* - Toby saw it _____
2 _____ of God.
It's about _____ boys who grow up in _____ .
What kind of film? _____
Where's it on? _____

listening challenge

4 Listen and circle the correct answer.

1 The film starts at 8.00 / 8.30.
2 They're going to meet at 7.45 / 8.15.
3 They're going to meet in a bar / at the cinema.

listen again with the **tapescript** *p.156*

5 **natural English** Listen. What's the pronunciation of *shall we?* Listen and repeat.

natural English
making plans together

When shall we meet?	Where shall we meet?
How about 8.00?	How about the station?
Fine.	Yes, OK.

6 Practise with a partner. Change the answers.

speaking it's your turn!

1 With a partner, complete the table about a film you want to see.

my kind of film!

name of film	_____
kind of film	_____
actors	_____
name of cinema	_____
times	_____

2 With your partner, write five questions to ask about a film. Then check with **lead-in exercise 2.**

3 Invite your partner to the cinema. Answer questions about the film, and plan when and where to meet.

What are you doing this evening?

Nothing. Why?

Well, do you want to ...?

4 Stand up. Invite another student to see the film.

can you remember ...

... two ways of inviting and responding, and two ways of making plans together? Write them down.

extended speaking
let's go out!

you're going to:

collect ideas	invent information	practice	role play
choose an activity you would like to go to	write information about your activity	ask and answer about your activity	invite others to your activity and arrange to meet.

 collect ideas

1 Choose an activity you would like to go to this weekend.
   – a concert   – a musical   – a sports event

2 Find a partner who chose the same activity.

 invent information

3 With your partner, invent information about your activity. Go to correct page.

   CONCERT: go to *p.127*   MUSICAL: go to *p.128*
   SPORTS EVENT: go to *p.125*

 practice

4 Work with your partner. A – invite B to your event. B – ask questions to get information. Arrange a time and place to meet.

   example   A What are you doing on ...?
             B Nothing much – why?
             A Do you want to come to ...?

 role play

5 Talk to at least two people who chose different activities.
   – ask them about their activities
   – invite them to go with you to your activity
   – if they say 'yes', decide when and where you are going to meet
   Complete the diary with the activities you are going to do.

6 Tell your first partner about your plans for this weekend.

DIARY

	activity:			meeting:	
	what?	where?	who?	when?	where?
Saturday afternoon	_____	_____	_____	_____	_____
Saturday evening	_____	_____	_____	_____	_____
Sunday evening	_____	_____	_____	_____	_____

thirteen review

grammar *be going to / might* + verb

1 What are you doing this evening? Tell a partner.

examples   I'm **going to** do some homework. (= sure)
I **might** see a film. (= possible)

2 Complete the table below with your plans.

WHEN	DEFINITE PLANS *I'm going to ...*	POSSIBLE PLANS *I might ...*
tomorrow	1	1
	2	2
next week	1	1
	2	2
next month	1	1
	2	2

3 With your partner, talk about your plans.

natural English

1 Circle the correct answer.

1   **A** What do you do / are you doing tonight?
B Something / Nothing much.
2   **A** Do / Would you like to go out tonight?
B I'm sorry, I can / can't.
3   **A** Where shall / do we meet?
B How about Alfredo's?
A Yeah, fine / well.

2 Check your answers using the **natural English** boxes in unit thirteen. Then practise the dialogues with a partner.

vocabulary verb + preposition

1 Complete with a verb from the left and a preposition from the right.

> look   spend   wait   pay
> speak   think   listen   agree

> with   after   to (x2)   on
> for (x2)   of

1   Why did you _____ _____ your teacher after class?
2   What do you _____ _____ his girlfriend?
3   Are you _____ _____ a phone call?
4   Do you _____ _____ a lot of music?
5   I _____ €200 _____ clothes at the weekend.
6   She _____ _____ their little boy when they went out to dinner.
7   How much did you _____ _____ your English dictionary?
8   I never _____ _____ my brother's opinions.

test yourself!

Now cover the REVIEW section and test yourself on unit thirteen.

test your vocabulary

From this unit, write down:

1   the missing prepositions:
listen _____ sb; agree _____ sb; spend money _____ sth; wait _____ sb
2   four more kinds of film: *thriller, ...*
3   time words / phrases from these jumbled letters:
TOHINTG
ROWTOROM
HIST KENEWED
TEXN EKEW

score   12

gap-fill

Fill the gaps.

1   **A** Do you _____ speak English outside class?
B Yes, sometimes.
2   **A** Would you like _____ go out tonight?
B Yes, great.
3   **A** Do you want to see that film?
B Yes, where's it _____ ?
4   **A** When _____ we meet?
B How about 7.30?

score   4

error correction

Correct the errors.

1   I going to phone my parents.
2   We might to see a film.
3   What do you do tonight?
4   I want to go there the next week.

score   4

total score   20

Look back at the unit contents on *p.103*. Tick ✓ the language you can use.

tick ✓ when you know this

natural English
- ☐ *How many times ...?*
- ☐ reacting to surprising information
- ☐ special greetings
- ☐ *have a* + adjective + noun

grammar
- ☐ present perfect (experience)
- ☐ present perfect and past simple

vocabulary
- ☐ opposites
- ☐ feelings
- ☐ fixed phrases

reading
that's incredible!

lead-in

1 **Think!** Are these sentences good, bad, or both? Why?

> I've never been to a dentist.

> I've broken my leg twice.

> I've run a marathon (42 kms).

> I haven't learnt to drive.

> I've lived alone several times.

> I've been in hospital once.

> I've never worked hard.

> I've been in love many times.

2 **natural English** Complete the sentences with words / phrases from **exercise 1**. Practise saying them.

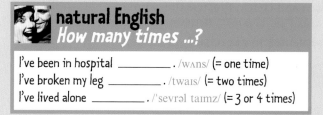
natural English
How many times ...?

I've been in hospital _____ . /wʌns/	(= one time)
I've broken my leg _____ . /twaɪs/	(= two times)
I've lived alone _____ . /'sevrəl taɪmz/	(= 3 or 4 times)

3 Tell your partner your ideas about **exercise 1**.

grammar present perfect

1 Look at the sentences in **lead-in exercise 1**.

1 <u>Underline</u> all the examples of the present perfect (*have / has* + past participle).

2 Are the sentences about *now* or *the past*?

3 Do we know *when* these things happened?

2 Complete the past participles in the table. Check with the verb list on *p.158*.

infinitive	past simple	present perfect (*have / has* + past participle)	
walk	walked	have / has ('ve / 's) haven't / hasn't	walked (REGULAR) _____ _____
play	played		
stay	stayed		
be	was / were		_____ (IRREGULAR)
break	broke		_____
run	ran		_____
drive	drove		_____
write	wrote		_____
see	saw		_____
meet	met		_____

3 Complete these sentences with the present perfect.

1 My best friend _____ _____ to England. (be)

2 I _____ never _____ abroad. (drive)

3 My teacher _____ _____ a grammar book. (write)

4 I _____ _____ to university. (be)

5 I _____ _____ *Gladiator*. (not see)

6 I _____ never _____ anyone famous. (meet)

4 (**14.1**) **pronunciation** Listen and check. Practise the sentences with the contractions (*'ve, 's, hasn't, haven't*).

5 Write questions for the sentences in **exercise 3**, like this:

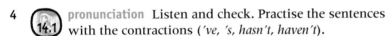

1   *Has your best friend (ever) been to England?*

6 Ask and answer with a partner.

go to **language reference** *and* **practice exercises** p.145

read on

1 Look at the pictures and read the first paragraph.
Do you think Ashrita has a normal life? Read the rest of the article. Were you right?

2 Read the article again. Then cover it and fill the gaps.

1 Ashrita is _____ years old.

2 He weighs about _____ kilos.

3 He has walked _____ kilometres with a milk bottle on his head.

4 At the moment he has more than _____ records.

5 He has broken more than _____ records.

6 He wants to push an orange for _____ mile with his nose.

Compare with a partner, then check in the article.

3 Underline the past participles in the article.

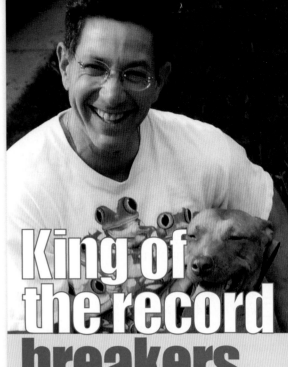

King of the record breakers

Ashrita Furman is 49 years old and lives in New York. In lots of ways he is very normal: he is 175 cms tall, he weighs about 75 kilos, and he works in a health food shop, where he is the manager.

In other ways Ashrita is not normal. He has travelled to every continent in the world, where he has done some unusual and **incredible** things. For example, he has walked 130 kilometres with a bottle of milk on his head (the longest distance); and he has juggled with three balls underwater for 48 minutes and 36 seconds (the longest time).

Currently he is in *The Guinness Book of World Records*, with more than twenty different **records**.

Why does he do these things? Firstly, Ashrita practises the Eastern art of **meditation**, and he believes that this training can give people the ability to do incredible things. But he isn't always serious about his records. Ashrita also wants to make people laugh with the things he does. For example, at the moment he is training to push an orange with his nose for one mile in the fastest time ever! In his life Ashrita has **broken** more than 80 **records**.

> **glossary**
>
> **incredible** (adj) /ɪnˈkredəbl/ difficult to believe
> **currently** (adv) /ˈkʌrəntli/ at the moment
> **record** (n) when sb does sth faster, longer, or better than anyone before
> **meditation** (n) thinking quietly to be calm (e.g. in yoga or T'ai Chi)
> **break a record** make / create a new record

Here are some more of his records.

CATEGORY	RECORD	WHEN?
Standing on a Swiss ball	the longest time: 3hrs 38 mins 30 secs	Dec, 2003
Pogostick jumping	the fastest mile: 12 mins 16 secs	July, 2001 in Oxford
Carrying a brick with one hand	the longest distance: 138 kilometres	Oct, 1999
Balancing glasses on his chin (for 10 seconds)	the highest number: 75 glasses	April, 2001

4 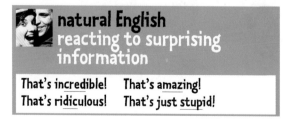 **natural English** pronunciation Listen and practise – copy the intonation.

natural English
reacting to surprising information

That's incredible!   That's amazing!
That's ridiculous!   That's just stupid!

5 Look at the pictures. What do you think of each record? Use the phrases in the **natural English** box. Tell a partner.

grammar present perfect and past simple

1 Look back at the article and answer these questions.
  1 When did he jump a mile on a pogostick?
  2 Where did he do that?
  3 When and how far did he carry a brick with one hand?

2 What tense is used in the questions in **exercise 1**? Why?

3 Underline the correct answer.

When we talk or ask about things in the past but we don't say when they happened, we usually use the present perfect / past simple.

When we talk or ask about things in the past and we say when they happened, we usually use the present perfect / past simple.

4 Complete the dialogues. Use the present perfect and past simple.
  1 A _____ you ever _____ to Korea? (be)
    B Yes, I _____ last year. (go)
    A Really? Where _____ you _____ ? (stay)
    B In a hotel.
  2 A _____ you ever _____ in hospital? (be)
    B Yes, when I _____ ten. (be)
  3 A I _____ never _____ to France. (be)
    B _____ you _____ to other countries in Europe? (be)
    A Yes, I _____ to Spain for a holiday last year. (go)
    B Where _____ that? (be)
    A Seville. It _____ fantastic. (be)

go to **language reference** *and* **practice exercises** *p.145*

speaking it's your turn!

1 With a partner, complete the questions in FIND OUT!

FIND OUT!

Have you ever studied _____?	Have you ever broken _____?
Have you been to _____?	Have you ever stayed in _____?
Have you driven _____?	Have you ever lived _____?
Have you met _____?	Have you seen _____?

Have you ever ...?

2 Interview different people using the questions above. If the answer is 'yes', you can ask *When ...?, Where ...?, Did you like it?*, etc.

  example A Cristina, have you ever done yoga?
           B Yes, I have.
           A Oh, when?
           B A few years ago.
           A Did you like it?
           B Yes, I loved it ...

can you remember ...

... the past participles of these verbs?

meet, be, break, learn, see, drive, write, run

wordbooster

opposites

1 Complete the opposites with words from the box.

forget	land	~~do badly~~	lose
miss	find	finish	fail

1 do well / *do badly* ____ in an exam, a test
2 pass / _____ an exam, a test
3 remember / _____ someone's name
4 lose / _____ your keys
5 start / _____ a book
6 win / _____ a football match
7 catch / _____ a train
8 planes take off / _____

2 What are the past tense and past participle forms of all the verbs?

feelings

1 Match the words with the pictures.

sad (about)
embarrassed (about) /ɪmˈbærəst/
frightened (of) /ˈfraɪtnd/
surprised (at) /səˈpraɪzd/
pleased (with) /pliːzd/
angry (with sb, about sth)
excited (about) /ɪkˈsaɪtɪd/
nervous (about) /ˈnɜːvəs/

2 Complete the sentences with words from exercise 1.

1 The children are _____ about the birthday party tomorrow.
2 He was _____ with me because I was late for work.
3 I was _____ he remembered my name. I've only met him once.
4 Small children are often _____ of the dark.
5 My manager is _____ with me – he says I'm doing well.
6 I was _____ when my girlfriend left. I really loved her.
7 I'm always _____ when my brother's driving – he's terrible.
8 I'm _____ when I forget people's names.

listening
how to ... say what you feel

can you remember ...

... eight adjectives describing feelings?
(Don't look at *p.114*.)

lead-in

1 **Think!** Look at the questionnaire. How do you normally feel in these situations?

How do you feel?

1 You're going on holiday tomorrow.   **excited**
2 Your holiday begins. You miss the train to the airport.
3 You're on the plane and it is now taking off.
4 You see your English teacher on the plane.
5 The plane flies through terrible weather.
6 The plane lands safely.
7 You get to the hotel. Your room is small and dirty.
8 You meet someone, fall in love, and then have to say goodbye on the last day of your holiday.

2 Stand up. Ask people how they feel.

> You're going on holiday tomorrow. How do you feel?

> I feel very excited.

> I'm quite nervous.

vocabulary fixed phrases

1 Circle the correct answer.

1 A I'm going to the Bahamas tomorrow.
   B Well, have a good time. / That's a shame!

2 A I passed my driving test this morning.
   B Don't worry. / Congratulations!

3 A We lost the match yesterday.
   B Oh, congratulations! / That's a shame!

4 A I've got a job interview tomorrow.
   B Well, good luck! / I'm really sorry.

5 A Sorry, I've lost your pen.
   B Oh, don't worry. / Thanks a lot.

6 A You've forgotten to bring my books.
   B Oh, that's great. / I'm really sorry.

2 **(14.3)** Listen and check.

3 **pronunciation** Listen again and copy the stress and intonation. Then practise with a partner.

4 **(14.4)** **natural English** Listen. Order the phrases you hear.

natural English
special greetings

☐ A Happy Christmas!   B Same to you.
☐ A Happy New Year!   B Thanks – you too.
☐ A Happy Birthday!   B Thank you!

5 Practise the dialogues, copying the intonation.

listen to this

tune in

1 Look at the picture. What can you see? Tell a partner.

2 (14.5) Read the questions, then listen to the start of the conversation.

1 What are their names?
2 What day is it?
3 What does the man give the woman?

listen carefully

3 Read the text, then listen to the whole conversation. Find three false things in the text.

The woman is going to England next week; she's feeling excited about it. She's frightened of travelling by plane because she's had several bad plane journeys. The man says she should ask her doctor for something to help her relax. She thinks that's a good idea.

listening challenge

4 (14.6) The man phones the woman after the journey. Listen.

1 Was the journey OK?
2 Was she frightened? Why / Why not?

listen again with the **tapescript** *p.157*

5 <u>Underline</u> phrases from **vocabulary exercise 1** in tapescripts 14.5 and 14.6 on *p.157.*

writing

1 Look at the cards. Match 1 to 3 with a to c.

a Aisha –
I was very pleased you got the job in Cairo. I hope you enjoy it very much.
Best wishes,
Alexander

b Hi Ronnie!
I hope you have a great day!
Love, Corinne

c Dexy
Great to hear you passed your exams – well done!
Have a fantastic holiday!
Love, Aunty Jan

2 **natural English** Read the box and find two phrases with the same meaning in the cards. Practise the dialogues with a partner.

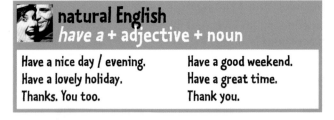

natural English
have a + adjective + noun

Have a nice day / evening.	Have a good weekend.
Have a lovely holiday.	Have a great time.
Thanks. You too.	Thank you.

3 What do you say in these situations?

1 it's Friday afternoon
2 someone is going to a party
3 someone is going on a journey
4 it's the end of the working day

4 With a partner, write two cards to different people in your class.

1 A 'good luck card' – decide what the person is going to do, e.g. go to university, move into a new flat, live abroad.

2 A 'congratulations' card – decide what the person has done, e.g. passed an exam, had a baby, got married.

5 Give your cards to the people. Do they like them?

can you remember ...

... six fixed phrases from the lesson?

example Good luck!

help with pronunciation and listening

listening listening to a song

> **Important!**
> Songs in English are a good way to practise listening. You can find the words of songs on the Internet – e.g. www.lyrics.com.

1 **In a song, the lyrics (= the words of a song) often *rhyme*.**

   examples   *four* /fɔː/ and *door* /dɔː/
   me /miː/ and *see* /siː/

   Find five pairs of rhyming words in the circle.

grows	end	go	you	bed
show	said	toes	depend	do

2 **Listen and complete the lyrics using the words in exercise 1.**

Love is all around

I feel it in my fingers, I feel it in my _____
Love is all around me, and so the feeling _____
It's written on the wind, it's everywhere I _____
(Ah, yes, it is)
So if you really love me, come on and let it _____
(Oh, yeah)
   chorus
   You know I love you, I always will
   My mind's made up by the way that I feel
   There's no beginning, there'll be no _____
   'Cause on my love you can _____
I see your face before me, as I lay on my _____
I kind of get to thinking, of all the things you _____
(Ah, yes, I do)
You give your promise to me, and I give mine to _____
I need someone beside me, in everything I _____
(Oh, yes, I do)
   chorus
Got to keep it moving, yeah, it's written on the wind
It's everywhere I _____ (yeah, yeah, oh)
So if you really love me, love me, love me
Just let it _____, come on and let it ...

pronunciation linking

1 **When a word ends in a consonant sound, and the next word begins with a vowel sound, you can join them together. Listen to the first verse again and notice the linking.**

   I feel‿it‿in my fingers, I feel‿it‿in my toes
   Love‿is‿all‿around me, and so the feeling grows
   It's written‿on the wind, it's‿everywhere‿I go
   (Ah, yes,‿it‿is)
   So if you really love me, come‿on‿and let‿it show

2 **With a partner, mark the links in these questions.**

   example   get‿up‿early
   Did you get up early today?
   Did you have an egg for breakfast?
   Did you drink a glass of milk?
   Did you get a train or a bus?
   Did you walk or drive to work?
   Did you work all morning?

3 **Listen and check. Then ask and answer with your partner.**

fourteen review

grammar present perfect and past simple

1 Complete the questions with a verb from the box.

> forget   miss   ~~lose~~   break   lose   leave   fail

HOW UNLUCKY ARE YOU?

Have you ever ...	_lost_ your house keys?	☐ yes ☐ no
	_____ a train or a plane?	☐ yes ☐ no
	_____ to take your passport on holiday abroad?	☐ yes ☐ no
	_____ an important test or exam?	☐ yes ☐ no
	_____ your bag on a train / bus?	☐ yes ☐ no
	_____ your arm or finger?	☐ yes ☐ no
	_____ a lot of money?	☐ yes ☐ no

---

2 Work with a partner. Ask the questions, and tick ✓ the yes / no boxes. If they answer 'yes', ask more questions, using *When ...? Where ...? Why ...?*.

A Have you ever lost your house keys?

B Yes, I have.

A Oh, when?

B It was last year. It was at 12.00 at night ...

3 What's your total?

SCORES

0–1 ✓ You're very lucky! Go and buy a lottery ticket!

2–3 ✓ Not bad! You win some, you lose some ...

4–7 ✓ Unlucky! Be careful the next time you go out ...

🖼 natural English and fixed phrases

1 Fill the gaps.

1 A I'm 21 today.	B Oh, happy _____ !
2 A Have a nice weekend.	B Thanks. You _____ .
3 A I've got an exam tomorrow.	B Really? Good _____ .
4 A Here's your book.	B Oh, thanks a _____ .
5 A I can't go to Paris – I have to work.	B Oh, that's a _____ .
6 A I'm going to get married.	B Wow! _____ !

2 Check your answers using the **natural English** boxes and vocabulary fixed phrases in unit fourteen.

vocabulary opposites

go to **pairwork** *p.127*

---

test yourself!

Now cover the REVIEW section and test yourself on unit fourteen.

test your vocabulary

From this unit, write down:

1 the missing verbs:
c _____ / m _____ a train;
w _____ / l _____ a football match

2 four feelings from these jumbled letters:
VONEUSR
PSLEEAD
SRUPEDRIS
FRNITEGHED

3 the missing words in these phrases:
_____ Christmas!; _____ luck!;
Happy _____ Year!; _____ worry.

score ☐ 12

gap-fill

Fill the gaps.

1 My sister _____ never lived in a village.

2 A I've got ten brothers and two sisters.
   B _____ incredible!

3 A I've passed my exams.
   B _____ !

4 A _____ a nice day!
   B Thanks. You too.

score ☐ 4

error correction

Correct the errors.

1 I've only seen her once time.

2 Has he ever learn to drive?

3 She hasn't never stayed in a hotel.

4 A Have you been to Cairo?
   B Yes, I've been there last year.

score ☐ 4

total score ☐ 20

Look back at the unit contents on *p.111.* Tick ✓ the language you can use.

---

pairwork

one review

numbers and the alphabet

bingo!

1 Complete the card. Write:
 - SIX more numbers from 1 to 50
 - SIX letters of the alphabet

G			13
	1	4	
17		E	
	29		K

2 Listen to your teacher. ~~Cross out~~ numbers or letters on your card.

 The first person to cross out one line, say **BINGO!**

 The first person to cross out two lines, say **BINGO! BINGO!**

3 Play the game in groups of four. One person is the 'teacher'.

two

wordbooster

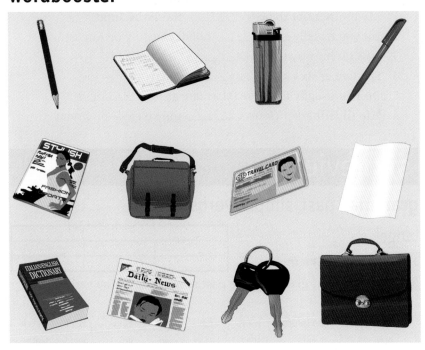

Look at the pictures with a partner. Which are Paula's things? Which are Christophe's things? Don't look at *p.18*.

> That's Paula's pen.

> Yes, and that's Christophe's lighter.

Check your answers on *p.18*.

two

listening

student A

Ask your partner.

1 What's the capital of Paraguay?
2 Where's Kiev?
3 What's an iMac?
4 How do you spell *dictionary*?
5 What's your teacher's family name?
6 What's the name of this unit?

two review

vocabulary personal things

Write the answers with a partner.
What's the answer to 11 down?

pairwork

two

listening

student B Ask your partner.

1 What's the capital of Peru?
2 Where's Krakow?
3 What's a Discman?
4 How do you spell *businessman*?
5 What's your teacher's first name?
6 What's the name of unit one in this book?

two review

vocabulary adjectives

1 B – write the opposites. Check with a partner

| expensive | quiet | easy | dangerous |
| cold | late | boring | terrible |

2 Work with your partner. Which adjectives from **exercise 1** go before these nouns?

| film | water | exercise | street |
| watch | book | party | train |

seven

reading

student B Read your sentences to your partner. Your partner says the negative.

example   A I went out yesterday
          B I *didn't go* out yesterday.

1 I got to work late.
2 We had lunch in the park.
3 They wanted to go.
4 He met me at the station.
5 She did her homework.
6 She grew up in Paris.
7 He went to the cinema last night.
8 I cleaned the flat yesterday.

three

wordbooster

student A Complete the clocks.

Tell your partner the time on all six clocks. He / She writes them down, e.g. 6.45.

Then compare your clocks and answers.

four review

vocabulary time phrases with prepositions

student B

1 My brother's birthday's _____ the 1st of June.
2 Do you usually go _____ holiday in July or August?
3 He's on his way to work _____ the moment.
4 See you at six o'clock _____ Sunday.
5 Do you usually have breakfast late at the _____ ?
6 The supermarket closes _____ nine o'clock on Friday.

six review

grammar past simple verbs

bingo!

1 Draw a grid like this:

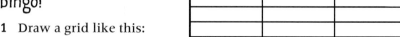

2 Complete your grid with the past tense of any nine verbs from the box.

| be (singular) | be (plural) | want | have | get | think | meet | watch |
| buy | clean | see | stay | do | go | decide | wash |

3 Listen to your teacher. ~~Cross out~~ past tenses on your card. When you cross out all nine past tenses, say BINGO!

4 Play the game in small groups. One person says the past tenses, the others cross them out.

four review

grammar present simple with frequency adverbs

1 Complete the phrases in column 1 using the pictures.

	alone	with my family	with a friend	with other(s) (who?)
I usually ...				
1 *have breakfast*				
2 _____				
3 _____				
4 _____				
5 _____				
6 _____				
7 _____				
8 _____				

2 **Think!** Tick ✓ the columns which are true for you.

3 Work with a partner. Talk about the questionnaire, like this:

A Who do you **have breakfast** with?

B I usually have breakfast alone.

A Oh, why?

B Because my family has breakfast after me.

A OK, and who do you **have lunch** with?

B With a friend at work.

five review

vocabulary food

1 Complete your part of the crossword.

CLUES DOWN ↓

1 a kind of fruit

2 you make toast from it

3 opposite of expensive

4 the restaurant is very _____

5 orange _____

6 🍵

9 you make this from milk

10 you pay this in a restaurant when you finish your meal

11 I get _____ and have breakfast

12 a list of things to eat in a restaurant

2 Read your clues to your partner. They write the answers in their crossword.

pairwork

three

wordbooster

student B

Complete the clocks.

Tell your partner the time on all six clocks. He / She writes them down, e.g. 3.30.

Then compare your clocks and answers.

eleven

reading

student A

Which is **cheaper** – the bike or the motorbike?

Which is **more difficult** to park?

Which is **faster**?

Which is **more practical**?

Which is **safer**?

Which is **better** for shopping?

Which is **more useful**?

five review

grammar countable and uncountable nouns

Work with the same partner for all these activities. For each question, write your time in column two.

Time trials!

		ideal time	your time	total
1	write the names of the things in the pictures	90 seconds	☐	☐ /20
2	tick ✓ the <u>un</u>countable nouns	45 seconds	☐	☐ /10
3	circle the nouns with *an*	30 seconds	☐	☐ /4
4	<u>underline</u> words with the /ʌ/ sound	30 seconds	☐	☐ /4
5	cross out words with the /ɒ/ sound	30 seconds	☐	☐ /2
	total	3 minutes	☐	☐ /40

Which pair got the best score?

seven

reading

student A

Read your sentences to your partner. Your partner says the negative form.

example   A   I went out yesterday   B   I *didn't go* out yesterday.

1   I saw her yesterday.
2   She became a doctor.
3   We left early.
4   They bought a new car.

5   He worked on Sunday.
6   They went to school.
7   She had chicken for dinner.
8   They got married.

three review

telling the time

1   (R3.1)   Listen. Draw the correct time on each clock.

1   2   3

4   5   6

2   With a partner, say the times in two different ways:

example   A   Four fifteen.
            B   Quarter past four.

eight

reading

student B

Work with another B student. Circle *much* or *many*.

1   How much / many people did the student ask for directions?
2   How much / many English did he speak?
3   How much / many food did he have for the journey?
4   How much / many water did he have?
5   How much / many people helped him?
6   How much / many money did he have in Scotland?

seven review

vocabulary appearance

student A

Describe your pictures. How are they different from B's?

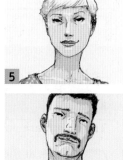

seven

reading

student A

Read this extra information about J K Rowling. Can you answer more questions in **grammar exercise 2** on *p.57*?

J K Rowling was born in 1965. When she was at school, she was friends with a brother and sister – their family name was 'Potter' and she liked the name very much. She studied French at Exeter University, and then she worked in London. After that she went to Portugal. She was there for three years, but she wasn't married for long, so she came back to Britain. She met a doctor called Neil, and they got married in 2001.

pairwork

vocabulary directions

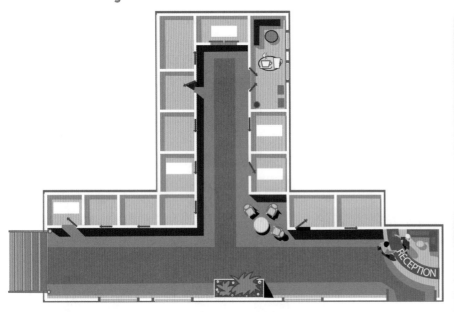

1 **R8.1** Look at the picture. You are at RECEPTION. Listen and follow the directions. Write the five places in the boxes.

2 Work with a partner. Ask and give directions to different rooms, like this:

A (you are near the lift) Excuse me, where's reception?

B Go along here and turn left …

nine

writing

2 You are at the Caterina Hostel in Budapest. Write an e-mail to your family.

Caterina Hostel
1066 Budapest V1, Teréz Krt 30

We are a small family hostel with friendly and helpful staff. We have private rooms, and the kitchen, toilets, and showers are all new this year. We are near Oktogon Square and only a few minutes' walk from the Opera House, the town centre, and the River Danube. Rooms, with breakfast included, for only $15. 24H reception and Internet access.

nine

reading

Youth hostels
Frequently Asked Questions

Do I have to share a room with other people?

Usually, yes. Most rooms sleep 2–4 people, but large rooms (for up to 10 people) are not very common now. In some hostels, you can get single rooms and family rooms.

Do I have to clean my room?

Normally you don't have to clean your room. Hostels ask you to be clean and tidy, and you have to hand in your dirty sheets when you leave. That's all. Most hostels also have a laundry where you can wash and dry your clothes.

Can I book a room in a youth hostel in advance?

Yes, you can normally book online for most hostels, and in the summer you often have to book in advance to get a room.

Are youth hostels only for young people?

No. You can stay in a youth hostel at any age. The only place that is different is Bavaria, in Germany, where you have to be under 26.

glossary

share (v) /ʃeə/ use or have sth with another person
common (adj) if sth is common, you find it often
tidy (adj) /ˈtaɪdi/ everything in order
hand in (sth) (v) give sth back

ten

listening

student A

1 **Think!** Read your situations.

SITUATION 1 You need to go to the airport this evening, but there's something wrong with your car. Tell B.

SITUATION 2 Listen to B, then offer to help.

SITUATION 3 You're in a restaurant with B, but you don't have any money. Tell B.

SITUATION 4 Listen to B, then offer to help.

2 Practise the situations in pairs. Begin like this:

B What's the matter?   A I ...

thirteen

extended speaking

SPORTS EVENT (e.g. basketball game, football match)

With your partner, complete the answers.

What?	_____
Who?	_____
When's it on?	*Saturday afternoon*
Where's it on?	_____
What time does it start?	_____
How much is it?	_____

nine

extended speaking

student A – hotel receptionist

Answer the phone:

Good morning, _____ Hotel. (your hotel name)

Listen and answer the caller's questions, and complete the booking form below.

name	_____
type of room	_____
dates	_____
caller's phone number	_____
caller's credit card number	_____

seven review

vocabulary appearance

student B

Describe your pictures. How are they different from A's?

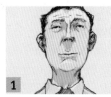

pairwork

ten

listening

student B

1   Think! Read your situations.

SITUATION 1: Listen to A, then offer to help.

SITUATION 2: You wrote a letter in English, but you think there are lots of mistakes in it. Tell A.

SITUATION 3: Listen to A, then offer to help.

SITUATION 4: You want to post some letters, but you have to stay at home for an important phone call. Tell A.

2   Practise the situations in pairs. Begin like this:

B   What's the matter?

A   I ...

ten review

vocabulary action verbs and parts of the body

student A

1   Answer the questions.

1   Is your hair on your head?

2   Can you put your finger in your ear?

3   Are your thumbs at the end of your legs?

4   Are your ears above your eyes?

5   Can you laugh and cry at the same time?

6   Do you wave with your hands?

2   Work with your partner. Don't show him / her your questions! Read your questions – your partner must answer.

twelve

wordbooster

With a partner, complete the text.

Terry tried to _____ his lawyer, Mr Donald, this morning. / The first time he _____ , / the line was _____ , / so he _____ again ten minutes later. / This time he got the _____ / and _____ _____ message / – *My name is Terry Brown / and my _____ 's 248 9936. / Could you _____ me as soon as possible, please?* / He waited for an hour / but his lawyer didn't _____ _____ , / so he _____ again. / Mr Donald was busy, / but Terry spoke to his secretary / and _____ another _____ . / Nothing happened. / He _____ again at 12.30 / but there was _____ _____ . / Mr Donald was _____ / – buying a mobile phone!

twelve

listening

student B

You phone BROWN'S PLASTICS to speak to your friend.

Think!

What's your friend's name?

What do you want to say to them?

examples come to my house this evening / meet me at 7.00 at the club

If your friend is out of the office, leave a message.

Write your phone number: _____

nine

extended speaking

student B – caller

You'd like to stay at A's hotel.

First, decide what you want:

type of room   ———————————

how many nights?   ———————————

dates   ———————————

Ask about:

the price

the price of dinner

facilities, e.g. parking, restaurant

Telephone the hotel, ask for information, and book a room.

thirteen

extended speaking

CONCERT (classical? pop? opera?)

With your partner, complete the answers.

What?   ———————————

Who?   ———————————

When's it on?   *Saturday evening*

Where's it on?   ———————————

What time does it start?   ———————————

How much is it?   ———————————

thirteen

listening

student A

Cineworld

Shall we dance (PG)

Love story / musical starring Richard Gere and Jennifer Lopez.

Lawyer John Clark (Richard Gere) isn't really interested in dancing, but then he sees beautiful dance teacher Paulina (Jennifer Lopez) and decides to go to her dance class ...

106 minutes

Showing at: 4.15   6.25   8.35

fourteen review

vocabulary opposites

1   Write opposites of the verbs.

> *example*   He <u>got on</u> at the wrong stop.
>
>   *He <u>got off</u> at the wrong stop.*

1   She <u>passed</u> the exam.

2   They <u>won</u> their last match.

3   She <u>started</u> the book yesterday.

4   I <u>remembered</u> his birthday.

5   When does the plane <u>take off</u>?

6   I just <u>caught</u> the train.

7   Where did he <u>lose</u> the money?

8   He <u>did well</u> in his exams.

2   Read a sentence to a partner. They must say the opposite sentence.

pairwork

ten review

vocabulary action verbs and parts of the body

student B

1 Answer the questions.

   1 Is your neck above your shoulders?
   2 Can you put your foot in your mouth?
   3 Are your toes at the end of your feet?
   4 Is your stomach below your feet?
   5 Can you sleep and smile at the same time?
   6 Can you pick something up with your teeth?

2 Work with your partner. Don't show him / her your questions! Read your questions – your partner must answer.

eleven

reading

student B

Which is **bigger** – the bike or the motorbike?

Which is **easier** to ride?

Which is **slower**?

Which is **more common**?

Which is **more dangerous**?

Which is **better** for old people?

Which is **more comfortable**?

thirteen

listening

student B

Arts centre

Collateral (15)

Thriller starring Tom Cruise, Jamie Foxx.

Tom Cruise plays a man who has to kill five people in Los Angeles in one night. Jamie Foxx is his very unlucky taxi driver.

120 minutes

Showing at: 3.30   5.40   7.50

thirteen

extended speaking

MUSICAL

With your partner, complete the answers.

Name of musical   _____

Who's in it?   _____

What's it about?   _____

When's it on?   *Sunday evening*

Where's it on?   _____

What time does it start? _____

How much is it?   _____

twelve

listening

student A

You are the telephonist at BROWN'S PLASTICS.

There's no one in the office at the moment. They're all having lunch.

When someone phones, you speak first.

Ask if they want to leave a message.

Complete the message.

Brown's Plastics

message for: _____

caller's name: _____

caller's phone number: _____

message: _____

_____

twelve review

vocabulary clothes

1 Complete the table with a partner.

clothes			
three things you wear on your feet	_____	_____	_____
three other things you wear below your waist	_____	_____	_____
six things you wear above your waist	_____	_____	_____
	_____	_____	_____
three things you wear above and below your waist	_____	_____	_____

2 **pronunciation** Work with your partner. Make rhymes using the words you wrote.

example a black *hat* /blæk hæt/ blue *boots* /blu: bu:ts/

1 a black _____   5 blue _____

2 a red _____   6 a dirty _____

3 brown _____   7 a hot _____

4 green _____   8 a nice _____

seven

reading

student B

Read this extra information about J K Rowling. Can you answer more questions in **grammar exercise 2** on *p.57*?

Joanne Kathleen Rowling was born in 1965. She went to Exeter University and then worked for Amnesty International in London for two years. After that she moved to Portugal and taught English. She left after three years and came back to Edinburgh because her sister lived there. She had a baby when she was in Portugal, and in 2003 her second child was born, this time a boy, called David. Then in 2005 she had a daughter, Mackenzie.

eleven review

vocabulary adjectives (3)

Find 10 more adjectives in the word square (vertical or horizontal).

Compare with a partner.

W	E	S	P	O	P	U	L	A	R
O	P	S	M	L	R	T	C	M	O
N	D	E	S	H	A	P	O	O	R
D	O	P	T	E	C	I	M	D	F
E	P	S	M	A	T	B	M	E	A
R	I	C	H	L	I	E	O	R	S
F	U	B	R	T	C	R	N	N	T
U	N	E	P	H	A	B	U	S	Y
L	U	C	K	Y	L	R	T	E	D

language reference

one

be positive and negative

You is singular (1) or plural (2, 3, 4, etc).
You use contractions when you <u>speak</u> English.

full form	contractions	negatives
I **am** a teacher.	I**'m** a teacher.	I**'m not** a teacher.
You **are** in room 10.	You**'re** in room 10.	You **aren't** (are not) in room 10.*
He **is** English.	He**'s** English.	He _____ English.
She **is** thirty.	She**'s** thirty.	She **isn't** (is not) thirty.*
It **is** a school.	It**'s** a school.	It _____ a school.
We **are** students.	We**'re** students.	We **aren't** students.
They **are** from Italy.	They**'re** from Italy.	They **aren't** from Italy.

* These contractions are possible:

They **aren't** from Italy. / They**'re not** from Italy.
He **isn't** English. / He**'s not** English.

go to exercises **1.1** *and* **1.2**

indefinite article a / an

Use *a* /ə/ before a consonant (*b, d, s*, etc.) sound.

a table	**a** student	**a** black taxi

Use *an* /ən/ before a vowel (*a, e, i, o, u*) sound.

an airport	**an** e-mail	**an** Italian passport

go to **exercise 1.3**

questions with be

The verb goes before the subject (*I, you, he*, etc.).

yes / no questions		short answers	negatives
Am I	in this class?	Yes, I am. (NOT I'm)	No, I'm not.
Are you	married?	Yes, you are.	No, you aren't.
Is he / she	a teacher?	Yes, he/she/it is.	No, he / she / it isn't.
Is it	difficult?		
Are we	in this room?	Yes, we are.	No, we aren't.
Are they	English?	Yes, they are.	No, they aren't.

Don't use contractions in short answers in the positive form.

NOT ~~Yes, I'm.~~ / ~~Yes, she's.~~

go to **exercise 1.4**

cover & check exercises

1.1 Complete the sentences.
Use contractions.

example He __'s__ from Italy. (+)
They *aren't* French. (−)

1 You _____ in my class. (+)
2 She _____ married. (−)
3 I _____ from New York. (−)
4 We _____ at university now. (−)
5 It _____ a London taxi. (+)
6 They _____ 21. (+)
7 He _____ my teacher. (−)
8 They _____ business students. (−)
9 I _____ a student. (+)
10 We _____ in class 2. (+)

1.2 Write the contraction in another way.

example We'<u>re not</u> teachers.
We *aren't* teachers.

1 He'<u>s not</u> married.
2 They <u>aren't</u> here today.
3 It <u>isn't</u> English.
4 We <u>aren't</u> doctors.
5 She'<u>s not</u> single.

1.3 (Circle) the correct answer.

example She's a /(an) American student.

1 She isn't a / an housewife.
2 I'm a / an engineer.
3 It's a / an big book.
4 He's a / an actor.
5 Is he a / an good accountant?

1.4 Order the words to make questions.
Answer the questions.

example a / you / are / student?
Are you a student? Yes, I am.

1 business/ she/ a / student/ is?
No, _____ .
2 are / from / England / they?
Yes, _____ .
3 he / married / is? No, _____ .
4 this / you / in / are / class?
Yes, _____ .
5 doctor / she / is / a? Yes, _____ .

have got (= have)

You use *have got* to talk about possession.

positive	negative
I / You / We / They **'ve** (have) **got** a car.	I / You / We / They **haven't got** a car.
He / She / It**'s** (has) **got** a printer.	He / She / It **hasn't got** a printer.

questions	short answers
Have you / they **got** a camera?	Yes, I / we / they **have**. NOT ~~Yes, I have got.~~
	No, I / you / we / they **haven't**.
Has he / she / it **got** a printer?	Yes, he / she / it **has**.
	No, he / she / it **hasn't**.

Remember:

's = is and *has*

He**'s** a doctor.	He**'s** got a computer.
is	**has**

go to **exercises 2.1** *and* **2.2**

singular and plural nouns

singular	plural	notes
book	books	most nouns → +*s*
pen	pens	
dictionary	dictionaries	*y* → +*ies*
country	countries	
bus	buses	*s, x, ch, sh* → +*es*
dish	dishes	
watch	watches	
person	people	irregular forms
man	men	
woman	women	
child	children	

natural English person / people /ˈpiːpl/

singular	plural
This **person** is from Thailand.	Who are these **people**?
Who's that **person**?	Those **people** are in my class.
	NOT ~~Those persons are~~

go to **exercise 2.3**

cover & check exercises

2.1 Write *'s*, *'ve*, *have*, or *has*.

1 Carol _____ got two phones.
2 We _____ got a big office.
3 _____ Tom got a Student's Book?
4 A _____ you got a pen?
   B Yes, I _____ .
5 My sister _____ got a TV and a computer in her bedroom.

2.2 Look at the pictures. Complete the sentences.

example He *'s got* a computer.

1 He _____ a printer.
2 He _____ a laptop.
3 He _____ a mobile phone.

4 She _____ a mobile phone.
5 She _____ a computer.
6 She _____ a digital camera.

7 They _____ a TV.
8 They _____ a CD player.
9 They _____ a laptop.
10 The laptop _____ a printer.

2.3 Write the plural form.

example briefcase *briefcases*

1 lesson _____
2 country _____
3 passport _____
4 class _____
5 businessman _____
6 nationality _____
7 magazine _____
8 person _____
9 family _____
10 box _____

this, that, these, those

	singular	plural
HERE (near me)	**this** book Is **this** your book?	**these** books Are **these** your books?
THERE (not near me)	**that** key Is **that** your key?	**those** keys Are **those** your keys?

Is this your bag?

No, these are my bags.

That bus?

No, those buses

go to **exercise 2.4**

possessive ′s

You use *′s* for possession.

John**′s** book.	NOT ~~the book of John.~~	Is this Mr Turner**′s** car?
That bag is Barbara**′s**.		My teacher**′s** name is Chris.

Remember, *′s* has three uses:

1 possessive	This is Jack**′s** magazine.
2 = *is*	My name**′s** Ella.
3 = *has*	He**′s** got two passports.

go to **exercises 2.5** *and* **2.6**

three

present simple (*I / you / we / they*)

To talk about things that are always true, or true for a long time:

I **come** from England.	They **don′t live** here.

To talk about things you often do / don′t do:

I often **walk** to school.
They **don′t read** a newspaper every day.

positive		negative	
I / You / We / They	**live** here. **study** English.	I / You / We / They	**don′t live** in Spain. **don′t speak** French. (don′t = do not)

questions	short answers
Do I / you / we / they **speak** English?	Yes, I / you / we / they **do**.
Do I / you / we / they **like** pop music?	No, I / you / we / they **don′t**.

go to **exercises 3.1**, **3.2**, *and* **3.3**

2.4 (Circle) the correct word.

example Is (this) / these your pen?

1 That / Those is my pencil.
2 This / These is my travel card.
3 This / These books are very useful.
4 That / Those e-mails are for me.
5 That / Those piece of paper isn′t yours.

2.5 In each sentence, is *′s* possessive, *is*, or *has*?

example That teacher′s class is in room 1.
   possessive

1 Where′s my travel card?
2 I think this is the doctor′s car.
3 My coursebook′s on the table.
4 Carol′s notebook isn′t here.
5 Carol′s got a French dictionary.

2.6 Write *′s* where necessary.

example Where are Marco͵things?

1 What is that actor name?
2 Have you got Anna rubber?
3 I think the green car is David.
4 When is your mother birthday?
5 **A** Is that your pencil?
   B No, it′s Mrs Taylor.

cover & check exercises

3.1 Complete the sentences with a verb.
example I _study_ English at school.

1 I _____ from Spain.
2 I _____ Spanish and English.
3 I _____ in Madrid.
4 I _____ in an office.
5 I _____ the train to work.

3.2 Make questions from the sentences in 3.1.
example Do you study English at school?

3.3 Make the sentences in 3.1 negative.
example I *don′t study* English at school.

wh- questions

What do you want?	**Who** are you?
Where do they live?	**Why** is she here?
How do you get there?	**How far** is it?
When do they start?	**How many** students are in the class?

go to exercises 3.4 *and* 3.5

like + noun/ + -ing

After *like* and *hate,* you can use a noun or verb + *-ing.*

I **like** Jack.	I quite **like** watching TV.
I **hate** football.	They **don't like** cooking.
Do you **like** Chinese food?	We **hate** shopping.

go to exercise 3.6

present simple (he / she / it)

positive	negative
He / She **lives** here.	He / She **doesn't work** in the bank.
It **starts** today.	It **doesn't stop** here.
	(doesn't = does not)

questions	short answers
Does he / she **speak** English?	Yes, he / she **does.**
Does it **go** to Oxford?	No, it **doesn't.**

spelling	notes
He works, She listens	+s
He goes, She watches, It does	+es
She stud**ies**	verb with one consonant +y → ies
He **has** NOT he haves	

go to exercises 3.7 *and* 3.8

3.4 Match the question words and answers.

1	Who?	a	Nine o'clock.
2	When?	b	In room 7.
3	Why?	c	Katherine.
4	How many?	d	Because it's good.
5	Where?	e	Ten.

3.5 Change the sentences into questions. Use a question word.

example I work in a bank.
   Where do you work?

1 I leave the flat at 7.30.
2 It's ten kilometres.
3 I play football because I like it.
4 I live in Budapest.
5 They get there by train.

3.6 Complete the sentences with an *-ing* form from the box.

~~play~~ study listen go live watch

example Do you like *playing* tennis?

1 We hate _____ TV.
2 I like _____ to music in the car.
3 I really like _____ English.
4 I like _____ out at the weekend.
5 Do you like _____ in the city?

3.7 Change the sentences to *she.*

example I work on Saturday.
   She works on Saturday.

1 I never watch videos.
2 I do a lot of work in the mornings.
3 I study German.
4 I go there a lot.
5 I walk to work.

3.8 Complete the sentences with words from the box. Then make them negative.

Germany wine fish tennis German ~~books~~

example He reads *books.*
   He doesn't read books.

1 She lives in _____.
2 He eats _____.
3 She plays _____.
4 He speaks _____.
5 She drinks _____.

four

present simple with frequency adverbs

Frequency adverbs (*always, usually, often, sometimes, hardly ever, never*) tell us how often something happens. They usually go:

after the verb *be*:

He **is always** late.	I **am often** here on Saturday.

after auxiliary verbs:

I **don't usually** see them.	He **can never** get to school early.

before full verbs:

She **often sleeps** in the afternoon.	I **sometimes work** at the weekend.

You can use some frequency adverbs at the beginning or the end of a sentence.

Usually he meets me at the station.	I work at the weekend **sometimes**.

go to **exercise 4.1**

possessive adjectives (*my, your,* etc.)

Possessive adjectives are the same with a singular or plural noun.

my book	**my** books

Remember:

use *his* when a man has something	use *her* when a woman has something

I often see **Mr Collins** and **his** dog.	I never see **Maria** and **her** brother.

subject	possessive adjective	possessive pronoun
I	**my** sister	This is **mine**.
You	**your** book	This is **yours**.
He	**his** car	This is **his**.
She	**her** brother	This is **hers**.
It	**its** name NOT ~~it's name~~	
We	**our** flat	This is **ours**.
They	**their** garden	This is **theirs**.

go to **exercise 4.2** (*go to the workbook, unit 7, for more information and exercises on possessive pronouns*)

cover & check exercises

4.1 Order the words to make sentences.

example often / works / late / he
<u>He often works late.</u>

1 tired / is / always / she
2 home / eight / usually / at / I / leave
3 listens / hardly ever / she / music / to
4 don't / Saturday / usually / they / work / on
5 never / home / before / I / six / get

4.2 Complete the sentences with a possessive adjective.

example **They** never use <u>*their*</u> car.

1 **We** can use _____ dictionaries in class.
2 **I** don't know _____ passport number. Do **you** know _____ number?
3 **Barbara** often forgets _____ books.
4 Do you know **Michael** and _____ sister?
5 It's a lovely dog, but I don't know _____ name.
6 **I** want to wash _____ hair tonight.
7 **They** work together. This is _____ office.
8 Give this to **Emma**. It's _____ homework.
9 I never understand **David** or _____ mother.
10 **Peter and Angela** live over there. Can you see _____ house?

Cover the grammar, then do the exercise. Check the grammar again to help you.

five

countable and uncountable nouns

countable nouns

Countable nouns [C] are singular or plural.

a book   some books   a sandwich   two sandwich**es**

uncountable nouns

Uncountable nouns [U] are usually only singular.

You can't count *bread*, *sugar*, etc. in English. NOT ~~one bread, two breads~~

(some) bread   (some) jam   (some) sugar   (some) milk
NOT ~~breads/ a bread~~

You can say:

a **piece** of bread / cake   a **cup** of tea / coffee   a **glass** of milk / juice

---

natural English coffee / a coffee

Normally *coffee / beer* are uncountable. In conversation, you can say
a coffee = a cup of coffee.

Have you got **any coffee**? = a packet of coffee
Would you like **a coffee**? = a cup of coffee
Can I have **two beers**, please? = two bottles or glasses of beer

---

go to **exercises 5.1** *and* **5.2**

some / any

	positive	negative	questions
	I've got ...	I haven't got ...	Have you got ...
singular	**a sandwich.**	**a sandwich.**	**a sandwich?**
plural / countable	**some rolls.**	**any rolls.**	**any rolls?**
uncountable	**some ham.**	**any ham.**	**any ham?**

go to **exercise 5.3**

cover & check exercises

5.1 Complete the table with words from the box.

~~orange~~ ~~apples~~ ~~coffee~~ milk sausages
cheese ham cornflakes apple butter
egg toast rolls sandwich jam

[C] Singular	[C] Plural	[U] Uncountable
orange	apples	coffee

5.2 Write *a / an* or *some*.

example I've got ___some___ bread.

1 Would you like _____ cup of tea?
2 I want _____ apples.
3 I've got _____ piece of cake.
4 I'd like _____ toast, please.
5 Would you like _____ apple or
_____ orange?

5.3 Circle the correct word.

example I've got ⓐ/ any student's book.

1 Have you got a / any bread?
2 We haven't got some / any pasta.
3 I usually have some / any toast for breakfast.
4 Has he got some / any brothers or sisters?
5 Do you want an / any apples?
6 I want some / any jam.
7 Would you like a / some ham sandwich?
8 I don't eat some / any butter.
9 Do you read some / any newspapers at the weekend?
10 I never buy a / any coffee.

can / can't + verb (possibility)

Can is the same in all forms: *I / you / he / she can (go)*.

| can = it's possible | can't = it's not possible |

Remember you can use *can* for requests (see *p.19*):

| Can I borrow your pen? | Can you open the window, please? |

positive	negative
You **can** /kən/ buy books here. NOT ~~You can to buy~~	You **can't** /kɑːnt/ buy bread here. (can't = cannot)

questions	short answers
Can /kən/ you buy wine there?	Yes, you **can**. /kæn/ No, you **can't**. /kɑːnt/

go to **exercise 5.4**

5.4 Write *can* or *can't* in the correct place.

> can't
> *example* You ⋏buy books in a bar.

1 What you eat or drink here?
2 You help me, please?
3 They understand you because they don't speak your language.
4 **A** She give you $100?
   B No, she.
5 He work on Saturday because he always plays football, but he work on Sunday.

---

six

past simple of *be was / were*

positive		negative	
I / He / She / It **was** You / We **were**	there yesterday.	I / He / She / It **wasn't** You / We **weren't**	there yesterday.
		(wasn't = was not; weren't = were not)	

questions		short answers	
Was I / he / she /it **Were** you / we	there yesterday?	Yes, No, I / he / she / it	**was.** **wasn't.**
		Yes, No, you / we	**were.** **weren't.**

go to **exercises 6.1** *and* **6.2**

past simple (1) regular and irregular verbs

Use the past simple for things that started and finished in the past.

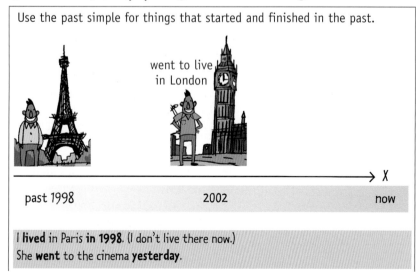

went to live in London

past 1998   2002   now   → X

I **lived** in Paris **in 1998**. (I don't live there now.)
She **went** to the cinema **yesterday**.

---

cover & check exercises

6.1 Write *was* or *were*.

1 We _____ very tired yesterday.
2 It _____ a beautiful day.
3 The people in the hotel _____ all French.
4 I liked the people at the party. They _____ very nice.
5 Susan _____ at work all day on Saturday.
6 _____ you at home last night?
7 The bread _____ cheap but the apples _____ very expensive.
8 My father _____ a doctor, but he doesn't work now.
9 What time _____ the first lesson this morning?
10 _____ your sisters at school in 1990?

6.2 Put the words in the correct order.

1 wasn't / Lucy / at / happy / very / school
2 late / class / we / for / this / morning / weren't
3 the / but / was / the / weren't / friendly / nice / waiters / food
4 film / interesting / wasn't / the / very
5 in / weren't / class / yesterday / why / you?

---

regular verbs		
I / You / He / She / It / We / They	liked it. worked there.	

spelling		
most regular verbs	add **-ed**	clean / clean**ed** watch / watch**ed**
verbs ending in **-e**	add **-d**	like / lik**ed** decide / decid**ed**
verbs ending in consonant **-y**	change **-y** to **-i**, and add **-ed**	study / stud**ied** marry / marr**ied**
most verbs ending in one vowel +one consonant (but not verbs ending in -y, -w, or an unstressed vowel, e.g. *open, visit*)	double the consonant	stop / stop**ped** plan / plan**ned** play / play**ed** open / open**ed**

irregular verbs
Many verbs are irregular in the past.

go to the **irregular verb list** *on p.158*
go to **exercises 6.3** *and* **6.4**

6.3 Write the sentences in the past.

1 I work in a bank.
  I _____ in a bank last year.
2 They play basketball on Fridays.
  They _____ basketball last Friday.
3 My father lives in Rome.
  My father _____ in Rome when he was young.
4 We study English at school.
  We _____ English at school.
5 She likes Michael's brother.
  She _____ Michael's brother.

6.4 Correct <u>one</u> error in each sentence.

                    went
example We ~~go~~ to the cinema last night.

1 I meet her brother last year.
2 He has eggs for breakfast this morning.
3 I think João was at home, but he wasn't.
4 She gets up at 9.00 this morning, so she was late for work.
5 I see him at the party last week.

seven

past simple (2) negative

negative form	
I / You / He / She / It / We / They	**didn't go** last night. NOT ~~I didn't went~~ **didn't stay** there. (didn't = did not)

go to **exercise 7.1**

past simple (3) questions

questions	
Did you / he / she / they **go** there? Why **did** you **stay** at that hotel?	NOT ~~Did you went there?~~

short answers
Yes, I / you (etc.) **did**. No, I / you (etc.) **didn't**.

go to **exercise 7.2**

cover & check exercises

7.1 Make the sentences negative.

example She lived in Japan.
  <u>*She didn't live in Japan.*</u>

1 They took the bus home.
2 She got married last year.
3 He left home when he was eighteen.
4 I grew up in Switzerland.
5 I studied German at school.

7.2 Complete the questions with a verb.

example **A** What <u>*did you have*</u> for dinner last night?
      B Steak. It was great.

1 **A** Where _____ on holiday?
  B To Rimini – it was lovely.
2 **A** When _____ your boyfriend?
  B In September, at a party.
3 **A** _____ TV last night?
  B No, I didn't. I did my homework.
4 **A** How long _____ for IBM?
  B Three years. I left in 2002.
5 **A** Why _____ the car?
  B Because it was very dirty.

zero article

When you talk about people / things in general, you don't normally use *the* with plural nouns or uncountable nouns.

Teachers work long hours.   NOT ~~The teachers~~ work long hours.
= teachers in general
Mobile phones are very useful.

go to **exercise 7.3**

object pronouns

Object pronouns replace nouns.

That's John – do you know ~~John~~ **him**?
Do you like this picture? I bought ~~the picture~~ **it** at the market.

subject pronoun		object pronoun
I		me.
You		you.
He	lived there.	him.
She	She knows	her.
It		it.
We		us.
They		them.

go to **exercise 7.4**

7.3 Make sentences using a word / phrase from each column.

example
Shop assistants don't get a lot of money.

~~Shop assistants~~	go shopping	at five.
Dictionaries	are nice	~~a lot of money.~~
Eggs	start school	at the weekend.
Museums	~~don't get~~	very useful.
People	aren't open	for breakfast.
Children	are	in the evening.

7.4 (Circle) the correct answer.

example   Did you see she /(her) yesterday?

1   He told I / me the answer.
2   I saw he / him in the bank yesterday.
3   Our aunt took we / us to the cinema.
4   Did you ask she / her for the money?
5   Why did you give they / them your books?

eight

how much / many?

You use:
how much with singular uncountable nouns;
how many with plural countable nouns.

uncountable	countable
How much money have you got?	**How many pens** have you got?
How much bread do you want?	**How many languages** do you speak?

In the answers, you often use *not much* with uncountable nouns, and *not many* with countable nouns.

How much money is there?

A lot.   Quite a lot.   **Not much.**   None.

How many books do you need?

A lot.   Quite a lot.   **Not many.**   None.

go to **exercise 8.1**

cover & check exercises

8.1 Write *How much?* or *How many?*

example   I've got some bread in the house. *How much?*

1   She speaks a lot of different languages.
2   We used a lot of petrol.
3   We need some more water.
4   I've got some oranges.
5   Rachel spent the money.
6   I bought some tea.
7   We met some people.
8   He's got quite a lot of pasta.
9   I sold the books.
10   She had some homework to do.

there is / are

You use *there is* and *there are* to say that something or someone exists.

There's a cinema near my house.   **There are** some shops in the village.
There's a table in the kitchen.   **There aren't** any dictionaries in the classroom.

You often use these structures before *a / an, some* and *any*.

nouns	positive	negative	questions
singular countable	There's a table.	There isn't a window.	Is there a key?
uncountable	There's some food.	There isn't any bread.	Is there any ham?
plural	There are some chairs.	There aren't any people.	Are there any books?

go to **exercise 8.2**

8.2 Complete the sentences with a phrase from the box.

There are some	There's a	~~There's some~~
There's an	There isn't any	Is there a
Is there any	Are there any	Is there a

example   *There's some* food on the table.

1 _____ park five minutes from here.
2 _____ milk in the fridge?
3 _____ e-mail for you.
4 _____ apples on the tree?
5 _____ dictionaries in the classroom.
6 _____ table in that room?
7 _____ dog in the garden?
8 _____ fruit.

nine

have to / don't have to / do I have to ...?

You use *have to* when something is necessary:

You **have to** go to school when you are a child.

You use *don't have to* when something is not necessary,:

You **don't have to** do homework every evening (but you can if you want).

positive		negative	
I / You / We / They	**have to** go.	I / You / We / They	**don't have to** go.
He / She / It	**has to** go.	He / She / It	**doesn't have to** go.
questions		short answers	
Do I / you / we / they **have to** go?		Yes, I / you / we / they **do.**	
		No, I / you / we / they **don't.**	
Does he / she / it **have to** go?		Yes, he / she / it **does.**	
		No, he / she / it **doesn't.**	

go to **exercises 9.1** *and* **9.2**

can / can't + verb (permission)

For form, see unit five on *p.136*.

You can use *can / can't* + verb to say something is or isn't permitted.

In most restaurants, you **can** drink wine. = it's OK, it's permitted
In most schools, you **can't** drink alcohol. = it's not OK, it's not permitted

Compare:

You **can** go now. = it's OK to go
You **can't** go now. = it's not OK, it's not permitted
You **have to** go now. = it's necessary to go
You **don't have to** go now. = it's not necessary, but you can go if you want to

go to **exercise 9.3**

cover & check exercises

9.1 Match rules a and b with examples 1 to 5.

a = it's necessary   b = it's not necessary

1 You have to work late tomorrow.
2 They don't have to study French, but they like it.
3 He doesn't have to work; he's got lots of money.
4 We have to study tonight – we've got a test tomorrow.
5 She doesn't have to do any homework for her English class.

9.2 Complete the sentences about restaurants with the correct form of *have to*.

1 In a café, you _____ pay the bill.
2 You _____ drink wine.
3 The waiter _____ serve your food.
4 The waiter _____ cook the food.
5 You _____ clean the table.

9.3 Tick ✓ the correct sentences. Correct the other sentences.

examples   We don't have ᵗᵒ work tomorrow; it's Sunday. ✗
            Can we go out tonight? ✓

1 You have to listen to the teacher.
2 Can I to pay you tomorrow? I haven't got any money.
3 You have to buy tea – we've got a lot.
4 He can go to the bank now – it's shut.
5 She don't have to work today.

ten

can / can't (ability)

For form, see unit five on *p.136*.

You can use *can / can't* + verb to talk about ability.

I **can** swim.	I **can't** drive.
Can you use a computer?	**Can** she play the piano?

Remember you can use *can* for requests (see unit two, *p.19*), for possibility (see unit five, *p.136*), and for permission (see unit nine, *p.139*).

go to **exercise 10.1**

something, anything, nothing, etc.

These mean the same:

someone = somebody

no one = nobody

anyone = anybody

Remember:

He said **nothing**. = He didn't say **anything**.

NOT He said anything. or He didn't say nothing.

	positive		negative		questions	
people	Someone Somebody	told me.	No one Nobody	came to class.	Did **anyone** **anybody**	come?
things	**Something** happened.		**Nothing** happened.		Did **anything** happen?	

go to **exercises 10.2** *and* **10.3**

natural English everyone

Everyone and *everybody* mean the same. Notice the singular verb after *everyone* (*has, knows,* etc.).

Everyone has a mobile now. NOT all people have...

She knows **everyone**. NOT she knows all people

I think **everyone** agreed with her.

go to **exercise 10.4**

cover & check exercises

10.1 Write five sentences about things Boris *can* and *can't* do very well.

example 1 *Boris can't swim very well.*

1 _____
2 _____
3 _____
4 _____
5 _____

10.2 Change the sentences using *anything*.

example I spent nothing.
I didn't spend anything.

1 He did nothing.
2 We bought nothing.
3 I saw nothing.
4 She drank nothing.
5 He told her nothing.

10.3 Complete the questions and answers.

example Did you see *anyone*?
No, *no one*.

1 Did he say _____? No, _____.
2 Do you know _____ in the class? No, _____.
3 Did she do _____ yesterday? No, _____.
4 Did you phone _____? No, _____.
5 Do you read _____ in English? No, _____.

10.4 Answer the questions using *everyone*, as in the example.

example Do they like it?
Yes, *everyone likes* it.

1 Do they know her?
2 Did you go out yesterday?
3 Do they have tickets?
4 Did they see the film?
5 Did you speak to her?

eleven

comparative adjectives

You use comparative adjectives with *than* /ðən/ to compare people / things.

 Tom Bill

Tom's **younger than** Bill.   Hotels are **more expensive than** youth hostels.
Bill's **older than** Tom.   Youth hostels are **less* expensive than** hotels.

* *more* is the opposite of *less*.

Remember: use *than*, not *that* with comparatives.

He's taller ~~that~~ **than** me.

One-syllable adjectives and some two-syllable adjectives:

adjective	comparative	notes
cheap	cheaper (than)	+*er*
safe	safer	+*r*
big	bigger	short adjectives ending in 1 vowel + 1 consonant: double the consonant + -*er*
easy	easier	change -*y* to -*i* +*er*

Many two-syllable adjectives, e.g. *useful, polite* and longer adjectives:

adjective	comparative	notes
tired	more tired (than)	-*ed* adjectives: use **more**
boring	more boring	-*ing* adjectives: use **more**
expensive	more expensive	
difficult	more difficult	

Irregular forms:

adjective	comparative
good	better (than)
bad	worse (than)

go to **exercises 11.1** *and* **11.2**

superlative adjectives

You use superlatives to compare people / things with all of their group. Use *the* with superlatives.

In my family, Uncle Jack's **the oldest** person, and Davina's **the youngest**.
Erica's **the most intelligent** person, and my brother Don is **the most practical**.

One-syllable adjectives and some two-syllable adjectives:

adjective	comparative	superlative	notes
cheap	cheaper (than)	**the cheapest**	+*est*
safe	safer (than)	**the safest**	+*st* short adjectives ending in 1 vowel
big	bigger (than)	**the biggest**	short adjectives ending in 1 consonant: double the consonant + -*est*
easy	easier (than)	**the easiest**	ending in -*y*: change -*y* to -*i* +*est*

cover & check exercises

11.1 Correct the errors. Be careful! Some forms are correct.

example   tired – ~~tireder than~~ *more tired than*
            bad – worse than ✓

1 small – smaller that
2 hot – hoter than
3 friendly – friendlyer than
4 fast – faster than
5 good – more good than
6 practical – more practical than
7 cheap – more cheap than
8 big – biger than
9 tall – more taller than
10 noisy – more noisy than

11.2 Write sentences using the key words.

example   my car / fast / your car
            My car's faster than your car.

1 Jim / nice / David
2 Tokyo / expensive / Paris
3 Water / good for you / coffee
4 Africa / big / South America
5 In cities, flats / common / houses

When you've finished an exercise, say the sentences aloud.

11.3 Order the words to make sentences. Begin with the word in bold.

example   book / in / the / exercise / difficult / **This** / most / is / the
            This is the most difficult exercise in the book.

1 in / shop / most / picture / bought / the / **She** / the/ expensive
2 of / the / I / part / city / in / cheapest / the / live
3 **It** / the / part / dangerous / the / town / most / is / of
4 shoes / shop / bought / in / most / **He** / the / comfortable / the
5 **Caroline** / school / the / girl / in / our / most / beautiful / was

Many two-syllable adjectives, e.g *useful, polite,* and longer adjectives:

adjective	comparative	superlative	notes
tired	more tired	**the most tired**	*-ed* adjectives: use **the most**
boring	more boring	**the most boring**	*-ing* adjectives: use **the most**
expensive	more expensive	**the most expensive**	
difficult	more difficult	**the most difficult**	

Irregular forms:

adjective	comparative	superlative
good	better	**the best**
bad	worse	**the worst**

go to **exercises 11.3** *and* **11.4**

should + verb

You can use *should* to recommend (= tell people what you think is good for them to do).

You **should go** to Green Park – it's lovely. NOT ~~You should to go ...~~
You **should see** that film – it's excellent.

positive	negative
I / You / He / She / It / We / They **should do** it.	I / You / He / She / It / We / They **shouldn't do** it.

questions	short answers
Should we **go** and see that film?	Yes, you **should.** No, you **shouldn't.**

go to **exercise 11.5**

11.4 Complete the sentences with the correct superlative form.

example She lives in <u>the nicest</u> (nice) part of the city.

1 Which is _____ (good) way to get to the station?
2 Is that _____ (expensive) bar in town?
3 Where is _____ (near) coffee bar?
4 That's _____ (bad) place to stay. It's very noisy.
5 Which is _____ (important) building in town?

11.5 Complete the sentences with verbs from the box.

go   watch   ~~stay~~   go   take   visit

example You should <u>stay</u> at the Carlton Hotel – it's wonderful.

1 You should _____ and see that new Spanish film. It's very good.
2 You should _____ the Taj Mahal when you're in India.
3 You should _____ to the Picasso Museum. It's really interesting.
4 You should _____ Sky News. It's on 24 hours a day.
5 You should _____ the train to Venice. It's a terrific journey.

twelve

present continuous

You use the present continuous:

1 to say what is happening now (at this moment):

past ————————→ now

My brother **is doing** his homework at the moment.
I can't phone my boss. He**'s driving** to Manchester.

cover & check exercises

12.1 Write the *-ing* form of these verbs.

1	leave	6	put
2	do	7	start
3	watch	8	stop
4	make	9	write
5	wait	10	sleep

Make a note of any differences between this grammar and your language.

2 to say what is happening around now (for a short period):

THIS WEEK

I'm staying with my aunt and uncle. (e.g. this week)
She's looking after their dog for a few days.

positive			negative	
I'm	studying.		I'm not	staying.
He / She / It's	working.		He / She / It **isn't**	working.
You / We / They're	eating.		You / We / They **aren't**	staying.

questions		short answers
Am I	**working?**	Yes, I **am**. / No, I'm not.
Is he / she	**listening?**	Yes, he / she **is**. / No, he / she **isn't**.
Are you / we / they	**waiting?**	Yes, you / we / they are.
		No, you / we / they aren't.

spelling

go *going*	say *saying*	drink *drinking*

BUT

smok<u>e</u> *smoking*	driv<u>e</u> *driving*	liv<u>e</u> *living*
swi<u>m</u> *swimming*	ru<u>n</u> *running*	si<u>t</u> *sitting*

vowel + consonant: double the consonant)

go to **exercises 12.1**, **12.2**, *and* **12.3**

present simple vs present continuous

You use the present simple:

1 to talk about things that are always true, or true for a long time.

I **come** from England.
She **works** in a school.
They **don't live** here.

2 to talk about things you often do or don't do.

I **walk** to school most days.
They **don't read** a newspaper every day.

For use of the present continuous, see above.

Compare:

He **wears** jeans <u>every day</u>, but <u>today</u> he**'s wearing** a suit.
He <u>often</u> **wears** jeans but he**'s wearing** a suit <u>at the moment</u>.
He <u>usually</u> **works** in his office, but <u>today</u> he**'s working** at home.

go to **exercise 12.4**

12.2 Correct the errors. Use the present continuous.

example   He ~~not~~ doing the exercise.
[isn't above "not"]

1 Where are you live now?
2 I don't working today.
3 They are siting in the kitchen.
4 He not having lunch.
5 They aren't study at the moment.

12.3 Make correct present continuous sentences.

example   What / you / do?
          What are you doing?

1 What / she / wear / today?
2 They / have / lunch / now?
3 I / not work / today.
4 We / not stay / long.
5 What / he / do / at the moment?

For a change, do an exercise orally with a partner.

12.4 Underline the correct answer.

1 It usually rains / is raining a lot in England.
2 My brother studies / 's studying very hard at the moment.
3 We go / are going to Spain every year.
4 I never play / am playing football in the summer.
5 I can't talk to my mother – she speaks / 's speaking to someone on the phone.
6 Three of the students come from / are coming from China.
7 What do you do / are you doing at the moment?
8 My sister always wears / is wearing jeans at the weekend.
9 A Where's Carlo?
   B He reads / 's reading something in the library.
10 My boss speaks / is speaking Japanese very well. That's very unusual for an English person.

thirteen

be going to + verb

You use *be going to* + verb to talk about things you plan to do in the future.

I**'m going to** buy a flat in the centre.
He**'s going to** work in Budapest in September.
He**'s going to** learn Hungarian.

past ——————→ now ——————→ the future

positive		negative	
I'm He / She / It's We / You / They're	going to do it.	I'm He / She / It **isn't** ('s not) We / You / They **aren't** ('re not)	going to do it.
questions		short answers	
Am I Are we / you / they Is he / she	going to do it?	Yes, I **am**. / No, I'm **not**. Yes, we / you / they **are**. No, we / you / they **aren't**. Yes, he / she / it **is**. No, he / she / it **isn't**.	

natural English *be going to + go*

When you say *be going to + go*, you don't have to repeat *go*.

I**'m going to** ~~go to~~ the bank this afternoon.
They**'re going to** ~~go to~~ Japan next year.
Are you **going to** ~~go to~~ the theatre tonight?

go to **exercises 13.1** *and* **13.2**

might + verb

You use *might* + verb to say that something is possible in the future.

I **might** go to Poland next summer. (= it's possible; I'm not sure)
They **might** stay in a hotel. (= it's possible; they aren't sure)

positive	negative
I / You / He / She / It / We / They **might** go.	I / You / He / She / It / We / They **might not** go.
We don't usually ask questions with *might*.	

go to **exercises 13.3** *and* **13.4**

cover & check exercises

13.1 Match the sentence halves.

1	Are you going to buy	a	get a new job?
2	What are they going to	b	work next year?
3	When are you going to	c	some milk?
4	Is she going to see	d	do after dinner?
5	Where's David going to	e	a film this evening?

13.2 Correct one error in each sentence.

1 Where's you going to live next year?
2 What's he going for do after school?
3 She not going to buy that car.
4 When does Julia going to Romania?
5 I'm no going by car; I can walk.
6 Are they going stay at home tonight?
7 **A** Are they going work now?
   B No, they not.
8 They're going to get married last year.
9 She going to learn Japanese next year.
10 James and Fred going to the cinema?

13.3 Write A or B against each of the sentences.

A the person is sure
B the person think's it's possible
example We're going to the bank. **A**

1 I might go out this evening.
2 She's not going to study English.
3 Martha might get married in July.
4 We might not go on holiday this year.
5 He's going to give us a test.

13.4 Put the correct form of *be going to* or *might*.

example I don't like bananas, so
     I *'m not going to* buy any.

1 It's raining a lot, so I _____ take an umbrella.
2 My son isn't sure what he wants to do. He _____ study economics, or perhaps politics.
3 We _____ see the concert on Saturday – I've got two tickets.
4 She hasn't got a watch, so she _____ be late.
5 I _____ go out, but I'm not sure.

fourteen

present perfect

You use the present perfect to talk about things that have happened in a time before (or up to) now. Usually we don't know <u>when</u> these things happened.

I've been to Greece.　　= before now. We don't know when.
He's worked in a restaurant. = before now. We don't know when.

We often use *ever* and *never* with the present perfect.

Have you **ever** been to Canada? = in your life up to now
I've **never** played basketball. = in my life up to now

Notice the difference between *have been to* and *have gone to*.

He **has been** to France. = Sometime in his life. He isn't in France now.
He **has gone** to France. = He went to France and is in France now.

positive		negative	
have / has + past participle		*have / has* + *not* + past participle	
I've		I	
You've	**worked** there.	You	**haven't worked** there.
We've	**seen** it.	We	**haven't studied** there.
They've		They	
He's		He	
She's	**been** there.	She	**hasn't done** it.
It's		It	

questions	short answers
Have you **seen** ...?	Yes I **have**.
Have they **spent** ...?	No, they **haven't**.
Has she **driven** ...?	Yes, she **has**.
Has it **rained** ...?	No, it **hasn't**.

For past participles, go to the **irregular verb list** on *p.158*

go to **exercises 14.1**, **14.2** *and* **14.3**

present perfect and past simple

You use the past simple for things that started and finished in the past. We often know when (or where) these things happened.

I **lived** in Paris **in 1998**.　　She **went** to the cinema **yesterday**.

You use the present perfect for things that have happened before (or up to) now. Usually, we <u>don't</u> know when these things happened.

Compare:

I've **lived** in Paris. = before now, we don't know when
I **lived** in Paris in 1998. = we know when, so you use the past simple

go to **exercise 14.4**

cover & check exercises

14.1 Write the past participle.

example　see　*seen*

1 eat　　　　6 do
2 live　　　　7 make
3 leave　　　8 break
4 go　　　　9 drink
5 run　　　10 forget

14.2 Make present perfect questions from the words.

example　he / ever / work / abroad
　　　　　Has he ever worked abroad?

1 she / be / to South America
2 he / ever / stay / in an expensive hotel
3 she / ever / break / her leg
4 he / read / many books in English
5 she / ever / write / a short story

14.3 Complete the dialogues.

1 A _____ you ever _____ (work) in Japan?
　B No, I _____, but I'd like to.
2 A _____ she ever _____ (break) her arm?
　B Yes, she _____, but it was a long time ago.
3 A _____ he ever _____ (make) bread at home?
　B No, he _____, but there's always a first time.
4 A _____ you _____ (eat) Thai food?
　B Yes, I _____. It's fantastic.
5 A _____ they _____ (drive) in America before?
　B Yes, I think they _____

14.4 Circle the correct form.

example　I (went) / have been to Germany last year.

1 She met / has met my uncle before.
2 Did you go / Have you been to the cinema last night?
3 What did you do / have you done last weekend?
4 I never met / have never met anyone famous.
5 They saw / have seen Jon at the airport yesterday.

tapescript

one

1.1
J Hello! I'm Jennifer.
M Hi, my name's Marc. Nice to meet you!
J And you.

1.2 tune in / listen carefully
J Hello! I'm Jennifer.
M Hi, my name's Marc. Nice to meet you!
J And you. Where are you from, Marc?
M I'm from France.
J Oh, right – and what part of France?
M From Paris, the capital.
J Oh, really? I love Paris.
M Yes, it's beautiful!
J So, are you a student here, then?
M Yes, I'm a student, I'm in my first year ... erm, what else ... I am twenty-one, and I'm single ...
J ... at the moment!
M So, Jennifer, are you a student too?
J No, I'm a teacher here.
M Oh! I'm sorry!
J No, that's OK – but I'm a new teacher here – I teach business.
M Oh, right, and are you American?
J No, no, I'm from Canada, from Toronto.
M Oh.
J Yes, and I'm here with my husband.

1.3 listening challenge
J Yes, and I'm here with my husband.
M Oh, with your husband?
J Yes, his name's Tim.
M And is he a teacher here too?
J No, no, well, he is a teacher, but not at the business school. He teaches English at the university.
M Oh, really? And is he from Canada too?
J No, he isn't. He's American, actually, from San Francisco.
M Oh, right, well ...

1.4
a housewife   a businessman
an engineer   a businesswoman
an office worker   a shop assistant
a waiter   an actor
a lawyer   a journalist
a police officer

1.5
These countries are in Europe:
France   Spain   Poland
Germany   Italy   Britain

These countries are in Asia:
Japan   China   Thailand

These countries are in South America:
Argentina   Brazil

1.6
French   Argentinian   Thai
German   Chinese   Polish
Japanese   Italian   British
Spanish   Brazilian

1.7
Chris's number is 042 694.
Simone's is 316 708.
Jane's is 372 241.
Kate's is 235 9978.
Gerry's is 084 5536.
And Charlotte's is 693 5887.

1.8
A Sue, what's your mobile number?
B It's 0779 242 1486.
A 0779 242 1486?
B Yeah, that's it.

1.9
3, 6, 9, 12, 15
15, 25, 35, 45, 55
7, 14, 21, 28, 35
70, 80, 90, 100, 110
60, 16, 50, 15, 40, 14
5, 15, 45, 135, 405

1.10
Are you a new student?
Where are you from?
What level's your English?
Who's your teacher?
Where's she from?
What's your room number?
How many students are in the class?
What nationality are they?

1.11
A Hi, Daniela, how are you?
B Fine. And you?
A Very well, thanks.

1.12
white wine   tea with lemon
orange juice   red wine
mineral water   diet coke
black coffee   hot chocolate

1.13
A Would you like a drink?
B Yes, a glass of white wine, please.
A OK.

1.14
A B C D
E F G
H I J K
L M N
O P Q
R S T
U V W
X Y Z

1.15
A Sorry, can you repeat that, please?
B Yes, sure.

A Sorry, can you play that again, please?
B Yes, of course.

1.16
R OK, that's fine then, so I need to take down some information about you.
S OK.
R Er, what's your full name, please?
S Susannah Clarke.
R Sorry, how do you spell that?
S S–U–S–A–double N–A–H C–L–A–R–K–E.
R Thanks a lot, and are you British?
S Yeah.
R OK, erm, sorry, I have to ask, how old are you?
S 27.
R And what's your address?
S 26 Cooper Road.
R C double O–P–E–R?
S Yeah.
R So that's Oxford – and your postcode?
S OX4 6JQ.
R Sorry, can you repeat that, please?
S Oh, OX4 6JQ.
R Thank you. And your phone number.
S 565688.
R Thanks, OK, that's all I need for now.

two

2.1

This weekend only – special prices at the Tech Shop! Our first special is the SYNTAC computer – down to a fantastic €680!

And come and see the CIBA laptop – you can watch your films on it when you want – normally it's €875, but this weekend, it's yours for 800.

Get the ENTEL printer for only €100 (A hundred?) – yes, that's right – €100!

And if you've got the computer and printer, get yourself a SONIC digital camera – this weekend, it's down to €95.

And at the same price, €95, get an eTone mobile phone – yes, only 95.

We've cut prices on CD players too – the SASSO CD player is only €20 – (How much?) Yes, half price, €20!

With the RJC widescreen TV down to only €500, and the EITO DVD player only €60 – go to the TECH SHOP this weekend. Offer ends Sunday!

2.2

A What's this thing?
B It's a DVD player.

A How many things are in the advert?
B Eight.

A This thing's fantastic.

2.3

A Have you got a mobile phone?
B Yes, I have.
A What make is it?
B It's a Nokia.
A Are you happy with it?
B Yes, it's fine.

A Has your brother got a computer?
B Yes, he has.
A Is it good?
B Yes, it's fantastic.
A Oh, really? What make is it?
B I think he's got an Apple Mac.

2.4

A What do you think of laptops?
B I think they're useful.
C I don't think they're necessary.
D I think they're expensive.

2.5

pencil	bag	rubber
notebook	travel card	newspaper
dictionary	piece of paper	pen
briefcase	course book	key
magazine	lighter	

2.6

The opposite of cheap is expensive.
The opposite of great is terrible.
The opposite of noisy is quiet.
The opposite of interesting is boring.
The opposite of difficult is easy.
The opposite of similar is different.
The opposite of safe is dangerous.
The opposite of hot is cold.
The opposite of early is late.
The opposite of dark is light.

2.7

A Can I look at your newspaper, please?
B Yes, here you are.

A Can I borrow your rubber, please?
B Yes, of course.

A Can you open the window, please?
B Yes, sure.

2.8

A Is this your dictionary?
B Yeah.
A Can I borrow it, please?
B Yes, sure.

A Is that your bag?
B Oh, yes it is – thanks!

A Are those keys Bruno's?
B I'm not sure.

A Are these books Julia's?
B No, they're Mark's, I think.

2.9 tune in

I haven't got my book.
What page is it?
Oh, I haven't got a pen.

2.10 listen carefully

T OK, everybody, now let's start – right, today's lesson is about the economy in Brazil, OK? Now, first of all, what's the capital of Brazil?
S1 Ooh, I can't remember …
S2 Oh, I'm not sure … is it Rio?
T Come on, David – what's the answer?
S3 Brasilia.
T That's right. Good. Now in your books, can you turn to page…
S1 Oh, sorry, I haven't got my book.
T Oh, never mind. Look at Mark's book, that's OK, so turn to page 27, OK, everybody? Good, now, …
S2 Sorry? What page is it?
T Page 27, Chris. Right, now, for this, you need to write.
S3 Oh, I haven't got a pen.
T That's OK, you can borrow this one. Here you are. OK, now let's look at the text, er, that's the first …

2.11 listening challenge

T OK, well, look, it's nearly 11 o'clock, so I think that's it for today.
  So for tomorrow, – a little homework – can you finish the questions in exercise 9 – then read pages 45 to 55 on Argentina.
S1 Do you want us to write the answers to the exercise?
T Yes, please – you can give them to me tomorrow. OK, everybody, see you tomorrow.
Ss Yeah. Bye!

2.12

A What's the capital of China?
B I think it's Beijing.
C I'm not sure.
D I can't remember.
E I don't know.

2.13

listen
repeat
Italy
remember
engineer

2.14

Can you complete the sentence?
Listen and repeat.
Remember to practise your English.
It's difficult to pronounce 'interesting'.
I don't understand the question.
How do you spell 'Japanese'?

2.15

Well, I've got one at home. I need it for work and for my studies too. It's quite small; I can put it in my briefcase, and it's white. It was very expensive, but I use it every day. I can write letters on it and send e-mails, and I can look things up on the Internet.

2.16

OK, I've got two of these at home. I've got one in my living room, and one in the bedroom. They're quite big – well, I've got a big one and a small one.

One is silver – that's the new one, and the other one is black – that's the old one.

OK, and you can turn it on or turn it off, and I watch it in the evening.

R2.1

A Can you turn off the TV, please?
B Yes, sure.

A Are these your keys?
B No, they aren't.

A Has she got a computer?
B Yes, she has.

A Can I borrow your dictionary, please?
B Yes, here you are.

A Have you got my newspaper?
B Yes, I have.

A Is this your father's bag?
B No, it isn't.

three

3.1
Towns and villages are places where we live.
Basketball and tennis are games.
Coffee and beer are types of drink.
Buses and trains are forms of transport.
Offices and factories are places where we work.
Rice and bread are things we eat.
Houses and flats are types of home.

3.2
C So, where do you live?
J I live in a small town.
C Oh, really? Where?
J Er, just outside London.
C Oh, that's good, and, and do you work there as well?
J No, I work in London.
C Where? What do you do?
J Well, I work in an office (ahh) in the city.
C So how do you get to work then?
J Well, I drive, because the office where I work has a car park.
C Oh, that's nice.
J Yeah.
C So what do you do when you're not working?
J I listen to music a lot.
C Oh, really? What, what kind?
J Well, classical mainly.
C And – anything else?
J Yes, I like a bit of hip hop.
C Oh, I like that too!
J Do you?

3.3
I play tennis a lot.
I drink a lot of water.

3.4
A Do you play tennis?
B Yes, I do.
C Do you study English at university?
D No, I don't.

3.5 tune in / listen carefully
A Hello?
B Oh, good morning. Is that Mr Roberts?
A Yes.
B Good morning, Mr Roberts. My name's Wendy Bolton from Bath City Transport.
A Oh, right.
B Have you got five minutes to answer some questions about transport in Bath?
A Er, yes, OK.
B Right, can you just confirm your address?
A Sure. It's 26 Kipling Avenue, and that's Bath, BA2 4PH.
B OK, thank you. And, what's your job?
A I'm a history teacher.
B Right. And where do you work?
A I work at the, er, King Edward School on North Road.
B How do you get to work?

A Usually by car.
B Ahh. Why is that?
A Well, because at that time of the morning, the buses are terrible (ahh).
B And how far is school from your home?
A Oh, I'd say about 3 miles.
B Three miles. So, when do you leave home in the morning?
A Usually at about 8.00.
B Right, so what time do you get to school?
A About 8.15.
B Thanks…

3.6 listening challenge
B Do you use your car a lot at the weekend?
A Well, I drive to the supermarket on Saturday morning, and er, oh, yes, to football on Sunday morning.
B Right. And do you use your car in the evening?
A Sometimes I go to the cinema and I'll drive there.
B What about public transport? Do you use that at the weekend?
A No, no, it's not very good really.
B Well, thank you, Mr Roberts. Thanks for your time.
A You're welcome.

3.7
Three o'clock
Ten past four
Five fifteen or quarter past five
Six thirty or half past six
Twenty to eight
Eight forty-five or quarter to nine

3.8
A Excuse me, have you got the time, please?
B Yes. It's quarter past three.
A Thanks.

3.9
travelling
skiing
computer games
cooking
going to the gym
driving
dancing
swimming
shopping
sightseeing

3.10
I really like dancing.
I quite like shopping.
I don't like computer games.
I hate football.

3.11
S You watch TV a lot. When do you watch TV?
M Oh, I watch TV every night, probably for about three hours.
S Right! You go shopping a lot. Where do you do that?
M I like to go to the local shopping centre. I really like shopping for food.
S Right. Er, you play football or rugby.
M No, it's football, actually. Yes.
S Football, right.
M I play with a women's team, about once a

week.
S And where do you do that?
M Oh, at the local football ground.

R3.1
A What time do you leave, Marc?
B About quarter past four.

A Euro Bank, good morning.
B Oh, hello, erm, is the bank open on Saturdays?
A Yes, we're open from 9.30.

Good evening, this is Peter Adams, and here is the news at 6.30.

A What time does the film start?
B Er, quarter past seven.

The next train on platform two is the 11.15 to Bristol.

A What time do you get to work?
B About quarter to eight.

four

4.1
H Well, I always get up at six-thirty, Monday to Friday (hmm), and then I have breakfast, of course.
P What time do you go to work?
H Erm, well, I leave home for work at 7.30, and then I get to work around 8.15, if the bus isn't late, sometimes a bit later.
P That's not bad.
H No.
P And lunchtime?
H Oh, well, yes, I usually have lunch about, well, between 1.00 and 2.00.
P And what time do you get home?
H I get home from work about six, and I have dinner early. I know this sounds really sad, but I hardly ever go out because I'm always tired in the evenings.
P What do you do?
H Well, I watch TV. Oh, and I often read the paper, and I never go to bed late. I'm always in bed before eleven.

4.2
I work about thirty-five hours a week.
I sleep about seven hours a night.
I watch TV about an hour a day.

4.3
January, February, …
July, August, …
April, May, …
Wednesday, Thursday, …
Sunday, Monday, …
Thursday, Friday, …
Spring, summer, autumn, …

4.4

father and son
brother and sister
girlfriend and boyfriend
mother and daughter
husband and wife
aunt and niece
uncle and nephew
grandmother and grandson
cousins
parents and children

4.5

A Have you got any brothers and sisters?
B Yeah, I've got a brother and two sisters.
A Have you got any cousins?
B No, I haven't.

4.6 tune in / listen carefully

G Have you got any brothers and sisters, Mandy?
M Yes, I have. Actually, I've got a twin sister, Carole, (hmm) and I've got another sister, Susie, she's 25, and then there's my brother, Michael. He's married, he's actually 34, and he's got two children, Lucy and Mark. (ahh)
G And what about the rest of your family?
M Oh, I've got a very big family, (hmm) I've got loads of aunts and uncles, and I've got about twenty-five cousins.
G Wow! And are you married?
M Yeah. I'm married to Damian, and we've got one little son – his name's David, and he's two.
G Ahh. And what does Damian do?
M He's an actor. (Oh?) He works mostly in er, radio.
G Ahh. And, and yourself? What do you do?
M Oh, I teach. I teach computer studies at the university, actually.
G Ahh, and er, what, what happens to David while you're at work?
M Well, I take him to my parents (oh) when I go to work, and they, they look after him.
G So I guess they live quite near you.
M Oh, yeah, about ten minutes away.
G Ahh. And, er, and your twin sister, Carole – do you see her often?
M Yeah! We live together.
G Oh!
M Yeah. Carole lives with Damian, David and me.
G Ah. Very close, then.

4.7 listening challenge

G Oh, right. So Carole lives with you?
M Yeah, she lives with me at the moment, because she can't find a flat. (ahh) She's got a boyfriend at last, though, and they want to get married next year and find a house together. (uh huh) We work together too.
G Oh, really?
M Yeah, at the university. (uh huh?) She teaches computer studies with me.
G So, not only is she your twin, (yeah) but you work together and you live together!
M Yeah! It's nice, actually. (ahh)

4.8

My sister and I live together.
My brother and father work together.
Can we have lunch together on Saturday?

4.9

sixth, seventh
fourth, fifth
twelfth, thirteenth
second, third
thirtieth, thirty-first
seventeenth, eighteenth
nineteenth, twentieth
first, second
third, fourth

4.10

fourth, seventh, Thursday, think
they, this, mother, brother

4.11

A Excuse me, have you got the time, please?
B Er, yeah. It's quarter past three.
A Thanks a lot.
B That's OK.

A Good morning. Barclays Bank. How can I help you?
B Oh yes, good morning. Erm, just an enquiry. Are you open on Saturday?
A Yes, we're open all day Saturday – from 9.00 to 4.30.
B Oh right. OK, thank you very much.
A You're welcome.

The train now standing at platform two is the delayed 8.15 to Oxford. This train now leaves at 8.20. We apologize for this delay.

A When does school start again?
B Well, I think it's the first of September.
A Are you sure? I think it's the third.
B No, ... it's the first.
A Yeah, you're right, it's the first.

five

5.1

ham, eggs, and sausages
cereals, coffee, and cornflakes
rolls, bread, and sugar
butter, toast, and cheese
tea, orange juice, and cake
bacon, honey, and jam

5.2

A What do you have for breakfast?
B I usually have toast.

A What do you have for lunch?
B I sometimes have a sandwich.

A What do you have for dinner?
B I often have pasta.

5.3

The /i/ sound: vanilla, chicken, fish, sandwich, chips
The /iː/ sound: cheese, peas, ice cream
The /ei/ sound: steak, bacon, potato
The /æ/ sound: apple, ham, sandwich

5.4

A What kind of soup have you got?
B It's onion or mushroom.

A What kind of ice cream do you like?
B Well, chocolate's my favourite.

5.5

C I have a brilliant Chinese restaurant near me. (Oh) It's really good food; the place is a little bit uncomfortable but the service is fast and it's very cheap. (Great!)
J There's a very nice French restaurant near me, the 'Pomme d'Amour'.
C Really?
J Hmm, 'The Apple of Love'. Yes, very friendly atmosphere and great food.
P Sounds great.

5.6

I can see him.
He can't meet you.
We can have dinner now.
You can't speak to her.
I can't leave now.
She can come for coffee.

5.7 tune in

W What would you like?
C I'll have chicken, please.
W OK. Anything else?
C No, that's all, thanks.

5.8 listen carefully

W Hi, how are you today?
C I'm fine, thank you.
W OK, what would you like?
C Hmm ... I think I'll have the chicken, please.
W OK, chicken ... and do you want potatoes or French fries with that?
C Er, let's see, er, I'll have the French fries.
W French fries, OK, and anything else? A salad, perhaps?
C Yes, do you have a green salad?
W Yes, we do. And what would you like to drink?
C I think I'd like some wine ... white? No, no, I'll have a glass of red wine.
W Glass of red wine – is house red OK?
C That's fine.
W OK, and large or small?
C Er, I'll, I'll have a large one as I'm not driving!
W OK, anything else?
C Er, no, no, that's all thanks. Oh, no, I'm sorry, er, can I have some water, please?
W Sure. Er ... still or sparkling?
C Still.
W Still. OK, no problem ...

5.9 listening challenge

W Is everything OK?

C Yes, it's really nice, thanks, and the chicken's very good.

W Good, pleased to hear it. Can I get you anything else?

C Er, yes, you can. Um, **can I have another glass of wine, please?**

W Sure. Red?

C Er, yeah, a, a small one this time.

W OK.

C Oh, er, yeah and **can I have some more water, please?**

W Yes, of course.

six

6.1

church   cathedral   palace
castle   bridge   fountain
statue   museum
square   market

6.2

A Erm, an hour was about right, and it was a very interesting tour.

B Well, the bus wasn't very comfortable, but erm, the tour guide was great.

C Well, the weather wasn't very nice, but we were happy.

D The people on the bus were all friendly, erm, and the driver was really funny.

6.3

I wasn't here yesterday.
She's very tired this morning.
The market was very interesting.
They were here last summer.
We weren't in the same class last year.

A Was Jack at home?

B Yes, I think he was.

6.4

Tom Cruise and Sean Penn are both actors.
They're both American.
Bill Clinton and Nelson Mandela were both presidents.

6.5

A How was your weekend?

B Oh, it was lovely. How was yours?

A Oh, it was terrible.

C How was your weekend?

D Yeah, it was nice. How was yours?

C Hmm ... a bit boring.

6.6

She wanted to go shopping.
I cleaned the house.
I played with my son.
We watched a video.
We stayed at home.

We played cards.
I decided to go for a walk.
I washed the car.

6.7 tune in

Juliet

T So, erm, how was your weekend?

J Oh, yeah, it was great. (Yeah?)

Tyler

F So, how was your weekend?

T We had a lovely weekend.

F Oh good.

T Yeah, it was nice.

listen carefully

Juliet

T So, erm, how was your weekend?

J Oh, yeah, it was great. (Yeah?) Er, I went to a party on Saturday night...

T Oh, yeah? Where did you go?

J (It was) at my sister's, and it was really good, and it's a long way, so I stayed the night there ...

T Oh, right ...

J then on Sunday morning, we went for a walk together and met one of her friends for lunch.

T Oh, yeah, nice.

J Yeah. How about you?

Tyler

F So, how was your weekend?

T We had a lovely weekend.

F Oh good.

T Yeah, it was nice. We stayed at home on the Saturday (yes) and on the Sunday we went and watched my son playing football.

F Oh, he plays football.

T He plays. He's not very good but he loves it. And when the game finished, we went home and watched a film.

F Ah.

6.8 listening challenge

Federay

T So, how was your weekend?

F We decided to go to the cinema.

T Oh yeah?

F Yes. On Saturday night the children stayed at home. (right) We bought our tickets online over the Internet. (Oh) We went to the cinema and we saw a lovely film.

T Oh, what was it?

F It was a very sweet comedy about a baby elephant.

6.9

Thursday the first of August.
I saw him early this morning.
What do you want to learn?
My daughter walked to the shops.
I bought some more coffee.
We start work at four-thirty.

6.10

C Hello, Deri.

D Hi, Conrad. Look, I'm, I'm really sorry I'm late.

C That's OK. No problem.

D I'm afraid the train was late. I mean, it left on time, (hmm) but er, at one point we were sitting still for forty minutes and ...

C Dear, oh, dear ...

6.11

C Hello, Deri.

D Hi, Conrad. Look, I'm, I'm really sorry I'm late.

C That's OK. No problem.

D I'm afraid the train was late. I mean, it left on time, (hmm) but er, at one point we were sitting still for forty minutes and ...

C Dear, oh, dear

D ... nobody told us why, erm, anyway we got to the station in Oxford and then there were no taxis, so eventually, I, I decided to walk here. (oh) Anyway, I'm, I'm really sorry.

C Look, it's fine. Let's get on with the meeting, shall we? Erm, ...

6.12

C Hello, Di!

D Hi, Carl, look, I'm sorry I'm late.

C That's OK, don't worry.

D I had to do some shopping, and there were so many people, and the queues were so long, and then I didn't have my credit card on me, and I didn't have enough cash, so look, I'm really, really sorry I'm so late.

C Look, don't worry about it, don't worry about it. What would you like to drink?

seven

7.1

I was born in 1965.
I grew up in a small village.
I left school at 18.
I went to university.
I became a teacher.
I worked in a school in Scotland.
I got married to an engineer.
I had a baby.

7.2

J Are the sentences true for you?

M Well, most of them, no. I wasn't born in 1965, and I didn't grow up in a small village. I grew up in Liverpool.

J What about your education?

M Different again. I didn't leave school at 18, and I didn't go to university. In fact, I left school at 16 and got a job.

7.3

She's tall, thin and quite attractive. She's got long, dark hair.

He's short and a bit fat, but quite good-looking. He's got short, brown hair, with a beard and a moustache.

She's quite tall and very beautiful. She's got medium-length, blonde hair.

7.4

A Erm, Do you want to see some photos?
B Yeah, yeah, let's have a look ... oh, who's that?
A Oh, erm, that's Mike – I work with him.
B Oh, right. Let's have a look at another one.
A That's Joe and Jenny – I work with them too.
B Oh, OK ... and who's that?
A Ah, er, that's my girlfriend.
B Oh, right! Very nice.
A Yeah, I, er, I met her last month.
B Hmm ... And who's that?
A Er ... that's me!
B No! That's not you!
A It is! Yeah, that's me!

7.5

She knows it.
Does she know him?
She doesn't know us.
She knows them.
She didn't know me.
Did she know her?
Does she know you?

7.6

B Who's that?
A Oh, that's Mike – er, I work with him.
B Oh, right.
A Yeah, he's my new boss.
B Oh, really? What's he like?
A Nice. Actually, he's quite funny.

7.7 tune in / listen carefully

Lynne

N Do you remember any of your school teachers?
L Oh, yes, erm, there was Miss Blake, at my secondary school.
N Oh, right, and what did she teach?
L She was a geography teacher (right) erm ...
N And what was she like?
L Well, she didn't look very attractive. Unfortunately, she had a bit of a moustache ... (right) and she was quite cold and strict and serious.
N Oh, right, and, and how long was she your teacher for?
L She was my teacher for about three years, I think.
N Right. Did, did you like her?
L Well, no, I didn't like her, but I respected her as a good teacher.
N Right, and when did you last see her?
L Oh, I saw her when I left school, about thirty years ago.

Glen

C Do you remember any of your teachers at school?
G Yes, yes, I do, yes. One in particular, lady, an older lady (right) – Rowena Robinson, she was called. (Oh!) Yes.
C Lovely name. What did she teach?
G She taught drama. (Right) And she would sing as much as speak, so it was always 'Good morning!' 'Hello!'
C How lovely! So what was she like?

G She was very, very, er ... well, she was very funny, (yeah) and, er, she was very old-fashioned, (right) and she liked people to speak properly.
C Yes. And how long was she your teacher?
G Oh, I think about er, four or five years.
C Hmm, did you like her?
G Very much, very much.
C And when did you last see her?
G I think it must have been about ten years ago.
C Ah.

7.8 listening challenge

T Do you remember any of your school teachers?
J Yes, I do. There's, er, one teacher, in particular, (yeah) Her name was Grace Benn, and, erm, she taught me English, and er, I remember her because she was very serious and clever (hmm) and interesting teacher, and (right) she really believed in me.
T Did, did you like her?
J Yes, I did, I, erm, I was, I was a little bit scared of her (hmm) because she was so strict, so serious, but, erm, I wanted to do well for her.
T Right, how, how long was she your teacher?
J For about two years, (right) she taught me for about two years.
T So, so when did you last see her?
J Oh, years ago (Was it?) I mean, this is ... twenty-five years ago, something ...

7.9

A When did you last see her?
B Oh, a long time ago.
A When did you last speak to him?
B Last week.

eight

8.1

L Oh, I got lost in Beijing in China.
N Oh, wow!
L Erm, I was looking for a hotel, (right) but the problem was I couldn't read the street signs ...
N Oh, because they were in Chinese ...
L Because they were in Chinese – and I was trying to ask other people (yeah) but having difficulties (hmm), and luckily someone helped me in the end, so it was all right, but it was about twenty minutes when I, I didn't know what to do!

8.2

A Excuse me, is this the way to the bus station?
B Yes, it is.
A Thank you.

A Excuse me, which way's the town centre?
B It's that way.
A Thanks.

A Can we get to the park along here?
B No, that's the wrong way.

8.3

OK, everybody, now, come here and stand next to the tape recorder, and bring your English coursebook with you.

Now, A students, go to the door, and take your books with you.

Right, now B students, go back to your chairs, and take your books with you.

Then come here again, and this time, bring your pen.

A students – go back to your chairs and sit down. Don't take your books – put them near the door.

B students – go to the door, pick up a book then take it to the correct A student.

Then go to your chair and sit down.

8.4

There's a table.
There isn't a table.
Is there a table?
Yes, there is.
There's some food.
There isn't any food.
Is there any food?
No, there isn't.
There are some chairs.
There aren't any chairs.
Are there any chairs?
Yes, there are.

8.5 tune in

A Excuse me, where's the coffee bar?
R It's on the second floor.

A Oh, excuse me. Is there a photocopier I can use?
R Yes, in the library.

A Excuse me, is there a lift here?
R No, I'm sorry, there isn't.

8.6 listen carefully

A Excuse me, where's the coffee bar?
R It's on the second floor.
A Thanks, erm, can I get some lunch there?
R Well, it isn't really a restaurant.
A Right. Can I get something hot?
R Erm, well, they have sandwiches, er, fruit, hot drinks – that sort of thing.
A Right. Not really what I was looking for. Erm, when does it close?
R Actually, it closes in half an hour.
A Half an hour. (hmm) Maybe I'll go into town. Thanks anyway.
R No problem.

S Oh, excuse me. Is there a photocopier I can use?

R Yes, in the library, but I'm afraid it's broken at the moment.

S Oh, is there another one somewhere?

R Well, there is one in the teachers' room but, erm, students can't just walk in and use it. Do you need to do a lot of copies?

S Well, not really, erm, it's just a homework exercise I'm working on.

R Right. How many copies?

S Just two.

R OK, well, I'll go and copy it for you. Erm, would that be OK?

S Of course, yes, thank you.

R That's all right. Come on, then.

8.7 listening challenge

A Excuse me, is there a lift here?

R No, I'm sorry, there isn't.

A Oh, I have to take all these books back to the library. Erm, it's on the second floor, isn't it?

R Hmm, yes, er, well, the stairs are over there. Erm, I could try and get some students to help you carry the books.

A Er, no, thank you, that's not necessary. How do I get there?

R OK, well, go upstairs to the second floor, (hmm) er, along the corridor, turn left and the library is the second door on your right.

A Second door on my right. Thanks.

R You're welcome.

8.8

/ʃ/ a Polish dictionary
/tʃ/ a French picture
/dʒ/ the German language

8.9

OK, so the food you can cook is fish, chips and sausages,
and then the sweet things you can eat are sugar, chocolate and orange;
the things in a town are station, church and bridge.
Right, and then the three countries are Russia, China and Belgium;
the jobs are chef, teacher and journalist;
and then finally, the three adjectives are sure, cheap and dangerous.

8.10

T Good morning, Trainline.

C Oh, good morning. I want a ticket to Liverpool, please.

T Right. Which station are you travelling from?

C From London.

T London Euston to Liverpool ... single or return?

C Single, please.

T Right, and which date would you like to travel?

C Er, Tuesday the 10th of June.

T Right. What time of day do you want to leave?

C Sorry, could you speak up, please?

T Yeah, of course. What time of day do you want to leave?

C Oh, erm, I want the 10.15 train.

T OK, the 10.15 arrives at 13.05. Good. Is it just one ticket?

C Er, yeah.

T Right, now, how would you like to pay for that?

C Oh, er, Visa card, please, er ...

8.11

A OK, so the Liverpool train leaves from Euston at 10.10 and arrives at...

B Sorry, could you speak slowly, please?

A Yes, sure. The Liverpool train leaves from ...

A If you want to travel before nine it's more expensive.

B Sorry, could you speak up, please?

A Yes, of course. If you want to travel before nine, it's ...

R8.1

A Erm, excuse me?

B Yes?

A Erm, is there a toilet on this floor?

B Yeah. Go along the corridor, turn right just there (hmm) and it's the second door on the left.

A Second on the left. OK, thanks very much.

A Hi, erm, where's Mrs Jackson's office? I think it's room 241?

B Erm, 241, OK, just go to the end of this corridor and it's the last door on the right.

A Oh, on the right, near the stairs?

B Yeah, just before the stairs.

A Thank you.

B You're welcome.

A Oh, hi. Is there a lift in this building?

B Er, yes. Go along here, turn right and it's at the end of the corridor.

A Lovely, thanks.

B That's OK.

A Hello, is the photocopy room this way?

B Yes, go along the corridor, turn right, and, er, it's on your right. It's opposite the toilet.

A Thanks.

B No problem.

A Excuse me, where's room 245?

B Erm, along this corridor, turn right, it's the second door on the right, next to the coffee bar.

A Great, thanks a lot.

nine

9.1

The credit card number is 4924 5680 3721 9609, and the expiry date is 12 / 08.

At 'Piece of Pizza', Spaghetti Carbonara is €7.20.

At the Hill Finders Hostel, a family room is £40 a night, and it's £3 extra per person for breakfast.

On the supermarket bill, butter's £1.10, and the tomatoes are 95p.

9.2

A Has the hotel got a bar?

B Erm, I think so.

A Is there a pool?

B I don't think so.

A Are all the bedrooms en-suite?

B I don't think so.

A Is the hotel near the centre of town?

B Er, I think so.

A How about breakfast – is it included?

B I don't think so.

A And have they got parking?

B I think so.

9.3 tune in / listen carefully

R Sandy Bay Hotel. How can I help you?

S Hello, could you give me some information, please?

R Yes, of course. What do you want to know?

S Well, how much is a double room for a night?

R When are you thinking of staying? During the week or at a weekend?

S Er, weekend.

R I'll just have a look ... erm, that's $100 a night.

S $100 a night, right, erm ... I've got a few more questions, if that's all right. Is breakfast included in the price?

R Yes, and it's a continental breakfast.

S Right, and the hotel is in the centre of town, erm so has the hotel got parking?

R Yes, parking's not a problem.

S And what about a pool?

R No, I'm sorry, but there is a public swimming pool near the hotel.

S Right, and do I have to pay a deposit?

R No, all you have to do is leave your credit card number.

9.4 listening challenge

S OK, well, that sounds fine, so I'd like to book a room, please.

R Very good. What date would you like to come?

S Next weekend – the 24th and 25th.

R Hmm, just the two nights?

S Yes, please, erm, Saturday and Sunday night.

R Good, and would you prefer a double or a twin?

S Erm, a double, please.

R And would you prefer en-suite?

S Yes, please, if possible.

R Not a problem. Can I have your name, please?

S Of course, it's Stephen Turner.

R OK, that's $200, Mr Turner. Can I have your credit card details?

S Yes, it's er, it's a Visa card, (hmm) and the number is 4929 ...

R 4929

S 8941

R 8941

S 3996

R 3996

C 0701.

R 0701. (hmm) Good, erm, and the expiry date?

S Oh, it's erm, it expires 10 / 09.

R Thank you. I'll just confirm the booking with you (hmm) – that's two nights, next Saturday the 24th and Sunday the 25th, a double room with ensuite.

S That's right.

R Thank you very much, Mr Turner, and see you next Saturday.

C Thank you! Goodbye.

R Bye bye.

9.5

R And would you prefer a double or a twin?

C Erm, a double, please.

R And would you prefer ensuite?

C Yes, please, if possible.

9.6

A We could call it 'Paradise Hotel'.

B Yeah, that's a good idea.

A And let's have a French restaurant.

B Hmm. I'm not sure about that.

ten

10.1

O The woman upstairs has got a new baby.

C Really? Is it a boy or a girl?

O A boy.

C Uhuh. What's he called?

O He's called Owen.

C Owen! Ah!

O He's very sweet.

C How old is he now?

O He's now ... three days old, I think.

C Gosh! And what does he look like?

O Just like his mum. His little button nose, and big, big eyes.

C Ah, sweet!

O Yeah, very cute.

C Does he cry a lot?

O Yes!

J Do you know any babies?

R Erm, yes, some friends of mine, Victoria and Tom, had a little baby girl (ahh) called Ruby.

J Oh, that's a lovely name.

R Erm, she must be about four, five months old now (hmm), she's er, she sleeps all the time still. Erm, lovely blue eyes when she does open them, and er, yeah, very cute.

J How often do you see her?

R Oh, about two, three times a week.

J Oh, right.

R Quite often.

10.2

I can swim very well.

I can swim quite well.

I can't swim very well.

I can't swim.

10.3

A Can babies swim at one year

B Well, no, they can't swim well until they're about two or three years old, (hmm) but they usually like being in water.

A Can children draw a circle when they're, say, two?

B Well, no, they can't – they can draw a circle when they're three or four.

A Can adults run five kilometres in an hour?

B Yes, and some people can run a lot more than five kilometres in an hour.

A Oh. Can cats stand on two legs?

B Yes, they can, but only if they hold onto something. They can't walk on two legs.

10.4

stomach and nose – the sounds are different

head and ear – they're different

thumb and back – they're different

toe and nose – they're the same

foot and tooth – they're different

shoulder and mouth – they're different

10.5

In situation 1, I think it's better to say something, because maybe you can help.

In situation 2, I think it's better to say nothing, because perhaps she doesn't want any help.

10.6 tune in / listen carefully

D Hello! Gran, it's me! Where are you?

G Hello, Darren. I'm here in the living room.

D Hello!

G Hello!

D How are you?

G Oh, I'm OK. I'm just watching the news. It's all bad today!

D Oh, dear, it often is, isn't it? (hmm) Oh, well. Erm, do you need anything?

G Erm, well, I haven't got any milk.

D Well, I'll get some from the shop.

G Oh, would you? (hmm) And also, I've got some letters to post.

D That's all right, I can post them on the way to the shop, can't I?

G Yes.

D Look, before I go, shall I make you a sandwich?

G Oh, yes, would you? Thank you – that's very kind of you.

D What kind of sandwich would you like?

G Oh, anything – I think there's some ham in the fridge – I'll come out to the kitchen with you and we'll have a look.

D OK, let's see ...

10.7 listening challenge

J Hi, Matthew.

M Hiya.

J Don't get up.

M Oh, ha, ha, very funny.

J How are you feeling?

M Well, my leg's OK – it's just that I'm a bit bored, really. I am reading lots of books, though.

J Oh ... poor boy!

M Hmm, but – there is one problem, erm, I really need my computer, but it's upstairs. I've got some work I need to do.

J All right, I'll bring it down.

M Ah, thank you. It can go just on that little table.

J OK. Shall I bring the printer down too?

M Er, no, it's OK – I don't need that.

J Shall I bring it down now?

M Yes, please.

J No problem.

M Ah, thank you. (hmm)

10.8

A I'll help you with the cooking.

B Oh, thanks very much.

A Shall I clean the bathroom?

B Yeah, thanks.

A Shall I make the coffee?

B No, it's OK, thanks.

10.9

house, about, mouth

group, spoon, tooth

double, country, couple

took, foot, would

10.10

I'll buy ... shall I ...?

could you ...? would you ...?

I can't do ... ..., do you?

10.11

I'm sorry we're not here at the moment. If you want to leave a message for Andy or Louise Roberts, please speak after the tone.

10.12

Message 1

Hi, Dad, it's me. Erm, can you help me? I can't do my homework, erm. Do you know all the countries in the EU? Can you have a think about that, and then, could you ring me on my mobile? Thanks a lot, Dad. Bye.

Message 2

Hi, darling, it's me. Look, I'm in town already. Shall I get the tickets for the cinema tonight? Erm, give me a call on the mobile, OK? Bye.

Message 3

Hi, Andy. It's Tom here. Erm, I'm at the bookshop, and you know that book on Japan that you're interested in? Well, they've got it, it's here, so I'll buy it for you and then I can get it to you when I see you tomorrow. All right? Bye.

Message 4

Mr Roberts, hello. This is Tara from the office. I'm just calling to remind you you've got a meeting tomorrow with Mr Tan. I'll book a table at the restaurant for you. Would you prefer Chinese or Thai? If you could let me know, that would be great. Thank you. Bye bye.

eleven

11.1

The bike is smaller than the motorbike.
The motorbike is more expensive than the bike.

11.2

A How long does it take to walk to the station?
B Not long.
A How long does it take to get to work?
B It takes about half an hour.
A How long does it take by scooter?
B It takes a long time.

11.3

A Bikes are safer than motorbikes.
B Yes, I agree with that.
C Hmm … it depends.

A Computers are more useful than TVs.
B Yes, that's true.
C Hmm … I'm not so sure.

11.4

butcher's	chemist
furniture shop	clothes shop
baker's	supermarket
shoe shop	department store
record shop	post office

11.5

N OK, can you give me the name of a popular sport?
D Erm, tennis.
N OK, good, and now can you tell me, what's a healthy drink?
D Orange juice.
N And what's your lucky number?
H Twenty-one.
N Oh great! Erm, can you give me the name of a modern building.
C The Guggenheim Museum.
N Now name a busy place for me.
H Piccadilly Circus.
N And give me a common name.
C Er, Peter.
N And now give me the name of a wonderful actor.
D Hmm, Tom Cruise.
N OK, now tell me a rich country.
C Er, United States of America.
N And lastly give me the name of a poor country.
H Erm, India.

11.6

You should go and see the new Johnny Depp film – it's great.

You should visit the Tate Modern – it's a fantastic art gallery.

Don't go to that new French restaurant – it's not very good.

11.7 tune in / listen carefully

P Hello, there, and welcome to this week's 'Travel Show'.
  Coming up in today's programme: do you go to the same place every year? Do you want some new ideas? Well, on today's show, our top travel experts recommend exciting places to go to on your holidays. So, from the very cheap to the very expensive, we've got plenty of ideas for you.

1 If you're getting married soon and planning your honeymoon, why not try Venice – probably the most romantic city in the world? The best time to visit is in the winter. There aren't so many tourists, so you can enjoy the city much more, and for me, the most beautiful view in the city is from San Marco to the church of Santa Maria della Salute. Winter is also the cheapest time to go (but not Christmas or New Year). A ride in a gondola is good fun, but the cheapest way to get around is by water bus – a vaporetto – that's what the locals do. Some of the nicest restaurants are in the Cannaregio area. There aren't many tourists there, so the prices are a bit lower too.

2 The best time to visit Crete is in late spring. It's warm enough to swim in the sea, but not too hot – the hottest time is July and August. You can travel around the island by bus, but if you want to see the most interesting places, then you should hire a car. You can do this in Iraklion, the largest town on the island, and it's not very expensive. While you're there, you should visit the Minoan palace at Knossos, near Iraklion. Then you could spend a few days in one of the quiet villages on the south coast, or drive up into the mountains. The other thing is the food is great – fantastic fruit and vegetables, fish straight from the sea, and retsina, the local wine.

3 If you want to visit a city with a difference go to Cairo. It's one of the most exciting cities in the world with fantastic monuments and museums to visit, and some of the cheapest shops you can find anywhere. You should go to Khan-el-Khalili, a very large oriental bazaar in the centre of Cairo.
  The quickest way to get around is a black and white taxi, but for me, the most relaxing way to see the city is from the river Nile. Take a ride on one of the traditional fishing boats called 'feluccas'. It's the perfect way to end a day spent sightseeing and shopping. But the best thing about Cairo is the people – they really are the friendliest people I know!

11.8 listening challenge

P Right, now, with me in the studio is Ben Robson, who is thinking about where to go on his next holiday. So, Ben, what do you think of the recommendations you've heard?
B Well, I'm sure Crete's lovely in summer, but, erm, we'll be going in winter, and I'm worried that there just won't be enough to do there, and that it won't be hot enough to go to the beach (hmm). Cairo, I've always wanted to visit, but my girlfriend went there last year (oh) – so that leaves Venice. I've been to Venice before in summer, and I loved it, so, er, seeing it in winter I think will be a very special experience.
P Fantastic!

11.9

It's the most beautiful place I know.
He's the oldest man in the class.
She's the best student.
That's the most expensive chair.
It's the worst place to eat in town.

11.10

P What do you think is the most interesting tourist attraction in New York?
R Erm, well, I like the Museum of Modern Art, (hmm) I like that a lot.
L I like the more touristy things, like Times Square (uh huh) and the Chrysler Building (oh!) – I thought they were great, because I'd seen them in movies, (hmm) and to see them in real life was fantastic. (hmm)
P What about the most dangerous area?
R Well, I suppose the obvious answer is Harlem, but I don't know.
L These days New York is so much safer and so much cleaner. I felt safe everywhere. I never went to Harlem but I felt safe downtown.
P And what about the most famous café or restaurant?
L Hmm. Joe's Café (hmm) in Greenwich Village is very famous, and well known apparently throughout the world. A real, New York coffee shop. (right)
R And I love the Rainbow Rooms. (Oh, yes) You can go up there and have a drink or a cocktail, and the views are fantastic.
P Hmm, hmm, so what's the busiest street?
R Fifth Avenue?
L Or Broadway, I think (hmm). It's very, very busy, with buses and cars and pedestrians.

R11.1

1 The River Nile is the longest river in the world. In total, it's 6,695 kilometres.
2 Everest is the highest mountain in the world. It's 8,848 metres.
3 Robert Wadlow is the tallest man in medical history. When he died in 1940, he was 2.72 metres tall.
4 Florence Griffith Joyner is the fastest recorded woman ever. In 1988, she ran 100 metres in 10.49 seconds.
5 The shoes are the most expensive shoes in the world. They cost two million dollars, and they're covered in 565 diamonds.
6 The rabbit is the world's biggest rabbit. He weighs 16 kilos and is called Roberto.
7 Jeanne Louise Calmant is the oldest woman in medical history. She lived in France and was 122 years old when she died in 1997.

twelve

12.1

R Have you got a group of friends you go out with?
P Yes, my old school friends. How about you?
R Yes, friends from work.
P How many are there in your group?
R Er, usually there's four of us.
P Hmm, are they all men, all women or both?
R Erm, there's er, three men and one woman.
P Hmm, are they all the same age?
R Roughly, roughly, yes.
P What sort of age are they?
R Erm, about my age really, (hmm) so, er, mid-thirties.
P Where do you go together, and what do you do?
R Well, we all love films (hmm) so we go to a cinema club together (right) and erm, watch, they're usually old movies.
P Hmm, and how often do you see them?
R Well, it happens once a month, so we usually meet up for a drink first, (hmm) and then go and see these films afterwards. (hmm)

12.2

A Have you got a group of friends you go out with?
B Yes – my old school friends. How about you?
A Yes, friends from work.

12.3

Sounds and music from the party (The Luncheon of the Boating Party)

12.4

Terry tried to ring his lawyer, Mr Donald, this morning.
The first time he called, / the line was engaged, / so he rang again ten minutes later. / This time he got the answerphone / and left a message/ :
'My name's Terry Brown/ and my number's 248 9936. / Could you ring me as soon as possible, please?' / He waited for an hour / but his lawyer didn't ring back, / so he phoned again. / Mr Donald was busy, / but Terry spoke to his secretary / and left another message. / Nothing happened. / He rang again at 12.30/ but there was no answer. / Mr Donald was out / – buying a mobile phone!

12.5

A Have you got a mobile?
B Yes, I use it mostly for work.

A When do you use your mobile?
B Mostly in the evenings and at weekends.

12.6 tune in / listen carefully

T Hello?
E Is that Tom?
T Yeah, speaking.
E Oh hi, Tom. It's Emma. How are you?
T I'm fine, thanks. How are you, Emma?
E Yeah, I'm fine, thank you. Is, er, Trisha there?
T No, I'm sorry, she's out.
E Oh, erm, do you know when she'll be back?
T Erm, I'm not sure – she went out at about ten o'clock. She's buying some clothes for a wedding next week.
E Hmm, she could be some time.
T Absolutely, she won't be back before lunch. Do you want to leave a message?
E Er, yes – Could you ask her to ring me?
T No problem. Any particular time?
E Oh, er, after 3.00?
T OK, er, has she got your number?
E No, I don't think she does, because it's my work number, so can I give you the number? (hmm) It's 642 1680.
T 642 1680.
E That's it. Thanks a lot, Tom.
T Pleasure. Bye, Emma.
E Bye.

12.7 listening challenge

R Good afternoon. Johnson Fabrics.
T Oh, good afternoon. Could I speak to Emma Waters, please?
R Er, yes, who's calling, please?
T Er, my name's Trisha Morgan – I'm a friend of Emma's.
R Right. Just one moment.
E Hi, Trish, how are you?
T Hiya, oh, I'm a bit tired, actually.
E You sound it. (Is) that from all your shopping?
T Erm, yes, it is.
E So, what did you buy?
T Well, it was a good shopping trip. I managed to get the dress, the hat and the shoes.
E Oh, that's terrific!
T Yeah, I know, I couldn't believe it. Erm, now listen, Tom told me that you rang this morning.
E Yes, I wanted to book the restaurant for Saturday but I couldn't remember the name.
T Ah, erm, it's called Browns, and erm, I've got the number here.
E Thanks.
T One moment ... hang on a sec, yep, here it is, it's 727 9946.
E That's terrific. Thanks so much, Trisha. Thanks for calling back.
T OK, I'll speak to you later.
E Take care. Bye bye.

12.8

R Good afternoon. Johnson Fabrics.
T Oh, good afternoon. Could I speak to Emma Waters, please?
R Er, yes, who's calling, please?
T Er, my name's Trisha Morgan – I'm a friend of Emma's.
R Right. Just one moment.

12.9

skirt	spell
trainers	problem
dress	stand
clothes	

12.10

Speak Spanish in Spain and South America.
Don't drink and drive.
Travel by public transport.
Eat brown bread for breakfast.
Practise your pronunciation every day.
Don't wear a skirt for skiing.
Stop sleeping and start studying.
Wear trainers when you're travelling.

12.11

Conversation 1

JL Excuse me.

M2 Yes?

JL I'm looking for the bus stop for the number 3.

M2 Ah, right, OK, you see the department store?

JL Sorry?

M2 That big shop there on the corner ...

JL Oh, yes.

M2 OK, turn left there and that's where the bus stop is.

JL OK, right – thank you very much.

Conversation 2

W Hello, erm, what would you like?

JL Hi, er, I'd like a black coffee.

W OK, and would you like anything to eat?

JL I'd like a ham sandwich, please.

W Right, OK, er, wholemeal bread?

JL Sorry? What's that?

W It's, it's like brown bread.

JL Ah, OK – what was that word?

W Wholemeal.

JL Wholemeal. OK!

Conversation 3

TO Good morning.

JL Good morning, erm, I'd like to go to the Victoria Art Gallery, please. Erm, what time does it open?

TO Yes, it opens at 10.00 and shuts at 7.00.

JL OK.

TO Oh, no, no, hang on a minute – I'm pretty sure it's not open at lunchtime.

JL Pardon? Could you repeat that?

TO Sorry, no, you can't go between 12.00 and 1.00, it's, it's closed for lunch.

JL Oh, I see, it closes at 12.00 for lunch. (hmm) Thank you very much. Goodbye.

TO Goodbye.

thirteen

13.1

A Is he going to learn the language?

B Yes, he is.

A Are you going to live there for a long time?

B No, I don't think so.

A I'm not going to get a job.

B Oh, right.

A Are they going to buy a house when they arrive?

B No, they aren't.

13.2

A What are you doing tonight?

B I'm going to see a film.

A What are you doing tomorrow?

B I might go shopping.

A What are you doing this weekend?

B Nothing much.

13.3

A Do you ever speak to your family in English?

B No, never.

A Do you ever eat Chinese food?

B Yes, often.

A Do you ever come to school by bike?

B Er, sometimes.

13.4

What's on at the cinema tonight?

What kind of film is it?

What's it about?

Who's in it?

Where's it on?

When does it start?

How long is it?

13.5

A Would you like to go to the cinema tonight?

B Yeah, OK.

A Do you want to go for a drink?

B Sorry, I can't tonight. Maybe tomorrow?

A Yeah.

13.6 tune in / listen carefully

T Hello?

G Hello, is that Toby?

T It is – who's that?

G It's Gina.

T Gina! Hi!

G How are you doing?

T I'm fine, fine, you know, working hard. How are you?

G Yeah, I'm fine too. Er, Toby, (hmm) are you free this evening?

T This evening? Erm, yes. Why?

G Well, would you like to go to the cinema?

T Yeah, great! What's on?

G Well, there's a film on called 'Collateral' ...

T Oh, no, I saw it last weekend. It's very good, though. Tom Cruise is fantastic.

G Hmm, yes. OK, what about 'City of God'?

T 'City of God'. What's it about?

G Well, it's a kind of thriller, erm, it's about two very poor boys, erm, who're growing up on the streets of Rio de Janeiro. (hmm) Erm, I've, I've heard it's fantastic.

T OK, where's it on?

G Er, the ABC.

T Right, no, great. Yeah.

G Oh, good.

13.7 listening challenge

T When does it start?

G Erm, half past eight.

T OK, let's meet at quarter to eight, and then we can have a drink first.

G OK. Where shall we meet?

T How about the bar next to the cinema?

G Right, good idea.

T OK, well, I'll see you later. Bye.

G Bye.

13.8

A When shall we meet?

B How about 8.00?

A Fine.

A Where shall we meet?

B How about the station?

A Yes, OK.

fourteen

14.1

My best friend's been to England.

I've never driven abroad.

My teacher's written a grammar book.

I've been to university.

I haven't seen 'Gladiator'.

I've never met anyone famous.

14.2

A That woman's got fourteen children.

B Gosh! That's incredible!

C Yeah, that's amazing!

A What's your dog's name?

B Cat.

A What?

B Cat.

A Oh, that's ridiculous!

C Yeah, that's just stupid!

14.3

A I'm going to the Bahamas tomorrow.

B Well, have a good time!

A I passed my driving test this morning.

B Congratulations!

A We lost the match yesterday.

B Oh, that's a shame.

A I've got a job interview tomorrow.

B Well, good luck!

A Sorry, I've lost your pen.

B Oh, don't worry.

A You've forgotten to bring my books!

B Oh, I'm really sorry.

14.4

A Happy birthday!

B Thank you!

A Happy Christmas!

B Same to you!

A Happy New Year!

B Thanks – you too.

14.5 tune in / listen carefully

A Hi Danny!

D Hello, Alison!

A Oh, good to see you.

D You too. Happy birthday!

A Thank you.

D How are you?

A I'm well, thanks.

D Good. Look, I've got a little present for you. Here you are.

A Oh, you shouldn't have ... how lovely! Oh, it's a book – about India. Oh, thanks a lot.

D That's OK.

D So when are you going to India?

A Oh, next week.

D Next week! Wow. You excited?

A Er, no, well, not really because I'm, well, I'm frightened of flying, especially, you know, when the plane takes off.

D Look, don't worry. It's a really safe way to travel.

A Hmmm, yeah, I know that but ... oh, I just get really nervous. I'm not sleeping at the moment.

D That's bad. (hmm). Have you ever had a bad plane journey or something?

A Hmm, yeah, once on a night flight. That was terrible.

D You should go and see your doctor, you know. He could give you some pills or something to help you to relax.

A Yeah, that's probably a good idea.

D Well, good luck, anyway. I'm sure it'll be fine.

A Yeah, I'm sure it'll be fine too. I can't wait, actually.

14.6 listening challenge

A Hello?

D Hi, Alison. It's Danny.

A Oh, hello, Danny! Wow! How are you?

D I'm fine, how are you?

A Great.

D How's the holiday going?

A Oh, it's just fantastic here.

D Good. And how was the plane journey?

A Oh, well, it was very long, erm ... but it was OK. I wasn't too nervous.

D That's great. So, why? What happened? Did you go and see your doctor?

A No, I didn't in the end, erm, but I actually met a very nice man who I sat next to on the plane and I just talked to him all the time.

D And that took your mind off it. Oh, that's brilliant! Well, look, I'll see you when you get back. Have a good time!

A Yeah, I will. Thanks for calling, Danny. Bye.

D Bye.

14.7

I feel it in my fingers
I feel it in my toes,
Love is all around me
And so the feeling grows,
It's written on the wind
It's everywhere I go,
ah, yes, it is
So if you really love me
Come on and let it show,
oh yeah

chorus
You know I love you, I always will,
My mind's made up by the way that I feel.
There's no beginning, there'll be no end
'Cause on my love you can depend.

I see your face before me
As I lay on my bed.
I kind of get to thinking
Of all the things you said,
Ah, yes, I do.
You give your promise to me
And I give mine to you.
I need someone beside me
In everything I do.
Oh, yes, I do.

chorus
Got to keep it moving, yeah,
It's written on the wind.
It's everywhere I go
Yeah, yeah, oh,
So if you really love me, love me, love me,
Just let it show,
Come on and let it ...

14.8

Did you get up early today?
Did you have an egg for breakfast?
Did you drink a glass of milk?
Did you get a train or a bus?
Did you walk or drive to work?
Did you work all morning?

irregular verbs

verb	past simple	past participle
be	was / were	been /biːn/
become	became	become
begin	began	begun
break	broke	broken
bring	brought /brɔːt/	brought
build /bɪld/	built	built
buy	bought /bɔːt/	bought
can	could /kʊd/ or /kəd/	been able to
catch	caught /kɔːt/	caught
come	came	come
cost	cost	cost
cut	cut	cut
do	did	done
draw /drɔː/	drew /druː/	drawn
dream	dreamt /dremt/ dreamed /driːmd/	dreamt/dreamed
drink	drank	drunk
drive	drove	driven
eat	ate	eaten
fall	fell	fallen
feel	felt	felt
find	found	found
fly	flew /fluː/	flown /fləʊn/
forget	forgot	forgotten
get	got	got
give	gave	given
go	went	gone/ been
grow	grew /gruː/	grown /grəʊn/
have	had	had
keep	kept	kept
know	knew /njuː/	known /nəʊn/
learn	learnt / learned	learnt / learned

verb	past simple	past participle
leave	left	left
lend	lent	lent
lose	lost	lost
make	made	made
mean	meant /ment/	meant
meet	met	met
pay	paid	paid
put /pʊt/	put	put
read /riːd/	read /red/	read
ring	rang	rung
run	ran	run
say	said /sed/	said
see	saw /sɔː/	seen
sell	sold	sold
send	sent	sent
show	showed	shown
shut	shut	shut
sit	sat	sat
sleep	slept	slept
speak	spoke	spoken
spend	spent	spent
swim	swam	swum
take	took /tʊk/	taken
tell	told	told
think	thought /θɔːt/	thought
throw	threw /θruː/	thrown /θrəʊn/
understand	understood	understood
wake up	woke up	woken up
wear	wore /wɔː/	worn /wɔːn/
win	won /wʌn/	won
write	wrote /rəʊt/	written /rɪtn/

Look at the **verb** column.
Cover the other columns and
test yourself.

iː	**ɪ**	**ʊ**	**uː**	**ɪə**	**eɪ**	ꞌ ꞁ ꜜ
/siː/ see mean	/sɪt/ sit English	/pʊt/ put foot	/tuː/ too you	/nɪə/ near beer	/deɪ/ day train	
e	**ə**	**ɜː**	**ɔː**	**ʊə**	**ɔɪ**	**əʊ**
/bed/ bed head	/əꞌbaʊt/ about teacher	/tɜːn/ turn first	/spɔːt/ sport more	/tʊə/ tour pure	/bɔɪ/ boy noisy	/gəʊ/ go slow
æ	**ʌ**	**ɑː**	**ɒ**	**eə**	**aɪ**	**aʊ**
/kæt/ cat Saturday	/kʌp/ cup double	/kɑː/ car half	/hɒt/ hot want	/ðeə/ there airport	/faɪv/ five my	/haʊ/ how south
p	**b**	**t**	**d**	**tʃ**	**dʒ**	**k**	**g**
/pen/ pen happy	/bæd/ bad rubber	/tiː/ tea butter	/deɪ/ day address	/tʃiːp/ cheap watch	/dʒɜːmən/ German Japan	/kæn/ can key	/gʊd/ good bigger
f	**v**	**θ**	**ð**	**s**	**z**	**ʃ**	**ʒ**
/fɔː/ four phone	/hæv/ have seven	/θɪŋk/ think both	/ðeə/ there father	/sɪks/ six class	/zuː/ zoo plays	/ʃuː/ shoe sugar	/ꞌtelɪvɪʒn/ television usually
m	**n**	**ŋ**	**h**	**l**	**r**	**w**	**j**
/mæn/ man summer	/nəʊ/ no tennis	/θɪŋ/ thing think	/heləʊ/ hello behind	/leg/ leg full	/red/ red wrong	/wiː/ we when	/juː/ you museum

chart © Adrian Underhill

OXFORD
UNIVERSITY PRESS

Great Clarendon Street, Oxford OX2 6DP

Oxford University Press is a department of the University of Oxford.
It furthers the University's objective of excellence in research, scholarship,
and education by publishing worldwide in

Oxford New York

Auckland Cape Town Dar es Salaam Hong Kong Karachi
Kuala Lumpur Madrid Melbourne Mexico City Nairobi
New Delhi Shanghai Taipei Toronto

With offices in

Argentina Austria Brazil Chile Czech Republic France Greece
Guatemala Hungary Italy Japan Poland Portugal Singapore
South Korea Switzerland Thailand Turkey Ukraine Vietnam

OXFORD and OXFORD ENGLISH are registered trade marks of
Oxford University Press in the UK and in certain other countries

© Oxford University Press 2006

The moral rights of the author have been asserted
Database right Oxford University Press (maker)
First published 2006
2011
10 9 8 7 6 5

ISBN: 978 0 19 438849 8

Printed in China

ACKNOWLEDGEMENTS
Project managed and edited by: Karen Jamieson
Designed by: Rebecca Crabtree

*The Authors and Publisher are grateful to those who have given permission to reproduce the
following extracts and adaptations of copyright material:* p.41 'Global breakfast / Round
the world at 8a.m.' by Amelia Gentleman / Emma Daly, The Guardian, 10 March
2002 © Guardian Newspapers Limited 2002. Reproduced by permission of
Guardian Newspapers Limited and Emma Daly; p.48 'I'm a guide' *Evening Standard*,
7th August 2000. Reproduced by permission of Solo Syndication Ltd; pp 112/113
'King of the Record Breakers', Ashrita Furman, www.ashrita.com/html.about/;
p.117 Love is all around Words & Music by Reg Presley © Copyright 1967 Dick
James Music Limited. Universal / Dick James Music Limited. All Rights Reserved.
International Copyright Secured. Phonemic chart reproduced with the kind
permission of Adrian Underhill and available from Macmillan ELT.
Sources: p.56 www.bbc.co.uk; pp.32 / 33 *The Independent*; p.96 www.morticom.com;
p.96 www.philipscollection.org

Although every effort has been made to trace and contact copyright holders
before publication, this has not been possible in some cases. We apologise for any
apparent infringement of copyright and in notified, the publisher will be pleased
to rectify any errors or omissions at the earliest opportunity.

Recordings directed by: Martin Williamson, Prolingua Productions.

Technical presentation by: Darrin Bowen, recorded at the Soundhouse Ltd.

Illustrations by: Claire Bretécher: (Agrippine character) pp.8, 10, 12, 13, 17, 19, 20,
21, 25, 28, 33, 36, 37, 41, 43, 44, 49, 52, 53, 57, 60, 65, 67, 68, 69, 73, 76, 81, 84, 85,
89, 91, 92, 97, 99, 100, 101, 105, 108, 113, 115, 116, 117 and cover illustrations
copyright © Claire Bretécher 2005; Fred Van Deelen pp.67, 124; Mark Duffin pp.6,
16, 39, 64, 85, 88, 116; Dominic Li pp.17, 31, 78; Joy Gosney pp.20, 22, 40, 42, 65,
90, 105, 119, 120, 122 131, 135, 138, ; Kveta pp.26, 63, 66; Martina Farrow pp.32,
58, 80, 81, 121; Belle Mellor p.117; Paul Oakley pp.19, 29, 32, 33, 68, 71, 107;
Jacquie O'Neill pp.83, 115; Gavin Reece pp.8, 18, 19, 62, 82, 91, 108, 119; Mathew
Vincent pp.50, 58, 84, 92, 111, 123; Philip Warner pp.66, 98, 101, 114, 131, 132,
134 136, 140, 141, 142, 143, 144.

*The Publisher and Authors would also like to thank the following for permission to reproduce
photographs:* Graham Abbey p.79 (baby laughing); Lina Ahnoff p.41(Moscow);
Alamy pp. 27 (Acestock / woman), 28 (Steve Skjold / Korean man), 47 (Peter
Mumford / woman and camera, Profimedia / church, Imagestate / Square, William
Owens / cathedral, Sarkis Images / Bridge, Alex Segre/museum, Jack Sullivan /
Market, Chad Ehlers / fountain), 74 (Michelle Chaplow), 79 (Profimedia / baby
sleeping/playing/waving); Allstar pp.106, 107 (Miramax Universal / 'Bridget Jones,
The Edge of Reason'), 127 (Miramax / 'Shall we dance?'), 128 (Dreamworks /
'Collateral'); Art Institute of Chicago p.97; Brand X Pictures p.79 (baby walking);
Bridgeman Art Library p.96 (Phillips Collection); BBC p.103 (Brighter Pictures);
Canon pp.15 (printer, digital camera); City Sightseeing p.48; Comstock Images
p.80; Corbis pp.27 (Russell Underwood / men drinking), 59 (Bill Miles / girl in b/w
top), 82 (Bettman / swimmer / woman), 94 (Lloyd Cluff / Nile), 109 and 125 (Icon
SMI / Jon Gardiner / basketball); Dawes p.87 (bicycle); Helen Birch Bartlett Memorial
Collection / Art Institute of Chicago p.97 (The painting by Georges Seurat, French,
1859–1891, 'A Sunday on La Grande Jatte', 1884); Digital Vision pp.10, 11 (sculpture),
75 (Rob Melnychuk / bedroom); Dorling Kindersley p.79 (baby holding bricks,
holding ball); Empics pp.9 (MokYui Mok / Pavarotti, AP / Mauro Alfieri / football),
28 (PA / Kim Myung Jung / sandwich bar), 56 (PA / Ian Westian / JK Rowling), 77 (PA /
Barry Batchelor/hotel at night); *Evening Standard* pp. 88 (woman rollerblading),
89 (man in sedan chair, man on electric scooter); Ashrita Furman pp.112, 113
www.ahrita.com/html.about/; Getty Images cover (Whit Preston / blue sky), cover
and throughout (Uwe Krejci / two people), pp.7 (Leland Bobbe / young man in
striped shirt), 9 (Image Bank / Yann Layma / Great Wall China), 21 (Zubin Shroff /
man), 23 (Image Bank / Terje Rakke / town, Kelvin Murray / office), 24 (Christian
Hoehn / man, James Darell / woman), 25 (Taxi / Dan Kenyon / man on phone),
28 (Image Bank / Ron Krisel / Spanish Girl, Herman Agopian / Turkish man), 31
(Uwe Krejci), 34 (Vince Streano / town), 42 (Foodpix / Laura Johansen / vanilla, Judd
Pilossof / fish), 51 (David Joel / woman on steps), 53 (Jerry Driendl / man, Taxi /
woman), 60 (Getty Images / maths teacher), 61 (Amy Neunsinger), 69 (Bruce Ayres
/ man, Marc Romanelli / woman), 85 (Greg Federman), 94 (Frazer Harrison / shoes),
99 (Jasper James / girl texting), 104 (Steve Smith), 108 (Image Bank / Marc Romanelli /
woman, Mario Tama / man); *The Guardian*, p.41 'Round the world at 8am' by Emma
Daly, *The Guardian*, 10 March 2002, © Guardian Newspapers Limited 2002.
Reproduced by permission of Emma Daly; Fereday Holmes p.52; Image Source
pp.65, 95, 100; Istockphoto pp.12 (orange juice, water, coffee, tea, chocolate, cola),
40 (churros), 42 (cheese, chicken, onion, apple, mushroom, steak, bacon, potato,
ham, chocolate, tomato, peas, strawberry), 47 (statue), 75 (breakfast), 79 (baby
crawling), 122 (butter, sugar, toast, ham, cheese, bread roll, sandwich, egg, sausage,
honey, tomato, mushroom, onion, strawberry, omelette); Karen Jamieson / John
and Jean Jacobs p.55; Jonathan Keeble p.52; Kobal Collection p.106 (Miramax /
'Chicago', MGM / 'North by Northwest', Dreamworks / 'Saving Private Ryan' /
'Shrek', Lucasfilm Ltd & Paramount / 'Indiana Jones and The Last Crusade',
Warner Brothers / 'The Shining'), 128 (Miramax / 'Chicago'); Alex McNaughten
pp.88 (girl rollerblading), 89; Nokia p.15 (phone); Damian O'Reilly p.35 (Mandy
and Carole together); Oxford University Press pp.12 (white and red wine), 16,
21 (girl), 23 (village), 25 (woman on phone), 28 (Jamaican girl), 30, 35 (Peter, Eve
and David), 40 (croissant, cabbage, porridge), 49 (Buckingham Palace), 59 (man in
red shirt, blue shirt, couple), 75 (man), 75 (Punchstock / Bathroom), 79 (baby
smiling), 122 (tea, orange juice, soup, apple); Alberto Paredes p.41 (Madrid);
Philips p.15 (TV, DVD player); Photofusion pp.60 (Geography teacher), 72, 79 (baby
crying); The Post Office p.9 (stamps); Juliet Prew p.52; Rex Features pp.6 (business
school / Tony Kyriacou), 9 (Ary Diesendruck / Carnival, Masatoshi Okauchi /
calligraphy), 23 (house, Sipa / factory), 27 (cinema), 34 (beach), 43, 45, 51 (man
washing car), 75 (gym), 77 (modern hotel), 91, 93, 94 (Everest, tall man, runner,
rabbit, Sipa Press / old woman), 106 (ITV / Mr Bean), 109 (concert, musical) 127
(concert); Robert Harding Picture Library pp.47 (castle, palace); Sony pp.15 (computer,
laptop, cd player); Stockbyte pp.7 (man in glasses); Suzuki p 87 (motorbike); Urban
Splash p.23 (Richard Cooper / Photoflex / flat); John Walmsley p.60 (Music and
Drama teacher); Zefa p.6 (M Thomsen / man), 75 (Brian Sytnyk / pool)

Commissioned Photographs: David Jordan: pp 7 (Jennifer), 11 (girls), 13, 35 (Mark,
Lucy, Michael, Karen), 37, 44, 79, 82, 98, 99 (girl on phone), 101, 102, 116; Mark
Mason: pp 12, 14, 18

With thanks to SAID Business School, Andy, Charlie and Madeleine Jamieson,
Alison and Adrian Reeve, Mandy and Damian O'Reilly, Carole Morrell, Rewley
House language school and Joe's Café in Oxford.

*The Authors would particularly like to thank the following readers and teachers for their help
with the initial research and piloting:* Martin Blaszk, Jo Cooke, Harriet Custance.
Rachel Dudley, Jane Hudson, Roger House, Roger Hunt, Amanda Jeffries,
Alexandra Kalmar, Liz Long, Sian Morgan, Dan parsons, Marisa Perazzo, Tim
Souster, Josie Reeder, Jo Savage, David Scott, Lyn Scott, Richard Sutton, Carol
Tabor, Louise Taylor, Veronika Toth, Kelley Tschetter, Michael Tschetter, Claire
Vickers, Louise Williams, Robyn Zayade, Anna Zurowska-Moroney, and the
teachers at International House, Bath and Edwards School, London.

The Publisher and Authors would also like to thank the following for their invaluable help: Mark
Appleton, Susannah McKee, Joanna Sosnowska, Michael Terry and Gaye Wilkinson.

The Publisher and Authors would like to thank: Martin Williamson for his enormous
contribution to the shaping of the listening material and to all the following
actors whose own ideas, anecdotes, and humour are such an important part of the
recordings: Candida Gubbins, Caroline Faber, Cate Hamer, Chris Rowe, Clare
Wille, David Michaels, David Shaw-Parker, DeNica Fairman, Federay Holmes, Glen
McCready, Hilary Maclean, James Goode, John McAndrew, Jonathan Keeble, Juliet
Prague, Juliet Prew, Lorelei King, Lynn Brackley, Nick Mercer, Nigel Greaves,
Patience Tomlinson, Paul Panting, Paul Tyreman, Phoebe Scholfield, Roger May,
Steven Pacey, Tyler Butterworth, Willow Nash, Yves Aubert